Powerful
Conversations

VOLUME 2

Powerful
Conversations

HOW TO TALK ABOUT
WHAT MATTERS MOST
IN WORK AND LIFE

VOLUME 2

KYLE MAJCHROWSKI

Printed in the United States

ISBN: 979-8-9867274-8-6

Produced in partnership with Kevin Johnson (kjbookcoach.com) and Richard Dodson (Richard-Dodson.com). Book cover and interior designed by Sue Luehring (sjldesign.carbonmade.com).

PRAISE FOR POWERFUL CONVERSATIONS VOLUME 2

From the very first pages, Kyle reminded us what true human connection feels like. As a leader in the construction industry, I strive to create transformational experiences for my teams and clients, and this book is a roadmap for doing just that. Kyle doesn't just talk about connection; he shows us how to live it. Practical, inspiring, and like an app for the soul, it challenges us to put down our devices and engage in conversations that truly matter.
— Ryan Heeter, West Division Leader for Gilbane Building Company

Building on the framework of the original, Powerful Conversations Volume 2 empowers readers to pick their own path through relatable stories and dive directly into engaging with their most pressing challenges and uncertainties. Most importantly, you don't have to do it alone. There's a chapter in here for everyone- find yours and share it with someone!
—Chris Ressler, Principal, Stantec

This book is a powerful reminder that meaningful leadership starts with meaningful conversations. Kyle doesn't just offer tools for engaging teams—he invites readers to reflect on how they show up for their families, their relationships, and themselves. A thoughtful and practical guide for anyone committed to growing with intention.
—Nick Caravella, AIA, Host of Wired to Build, Sr. Dir. of Growth at Cumulus

Powerful Conversations 2 goes even deeper into what it means to truly connect with people in a world that has become transactional and disconnected. Kyle reminds us that while we're becoming more efficient in today's world, more and more we're losing the human connection. What stood out to me is how much this book focuses on simply noticing people, slowing down enough to see them and treat them as more than just a task. The stories are relatable, and they highlight how being present can make a meaningful difference. This book reinforces that culture isn't built through systems or titles, but by human conversations that lead to stronger relationships and trust. Powerful Conversations 2 is a great reminder that real connection doesn't require big gestures. It starts with intention, attention, and the willingness to engage with people as people.
—Clint Welch, Intech Mechanical, Plumbing & Mechanical Trade Partner

I have lost track of how many of Kyle's first Powerful Conversations books I have given to people I care about, and I cannot wait for others to get their hands on his second book, Powerful Conversations 2! Once again, in his very honest way, he continues to guide you through a journey of self-discovery and transformation. His profound but discernible exploration of topics awakens the confidence and conviction in individuals to go out into the world and intentionally bring people together! His books are guidelines that you can periodically revisit to recenter yourself and relink that path to establish meaningful connections with others in personal and professional circles. I have personally discovered that the positive impact can happen at any level of our careers, independent from any special titles!"
—Margarita de Monterrosa, AIA, Senior Associate, Stantec

This book cuts through the noise and gets to the heart of what truly moves people and teams forward. Kyle blends honest stories with practical insight, reminding us that meaningful conversations aren't a "nice to have"—they're how real progress happens. This is a book for leaders and doers who value authenticity, connection, and action over theories and buzzwords.
—Mark Bokhoven, Preconstruction Executive, Swinerton

In healthcare architecture, outcomes depend on how well diverse teams think, decide, and communicate under pressure. Powerful Conversations provides leaders with a clear, human-centered framework for building cultures where people know and respect one another, making hard problems easier to solve without burning teams out. It is an essential read for anyone serious about aligning purpose, accountability, and respect for people.
—Eric Ubersax, Senior Project Manager, Devenney Group

As humans we crave connection and communication. This book provides the tools through the collection of topics to strengthen relationships, foster trust, and create authentic connections in personal and professional settings. Throughout the years Kyle has challenged those around him to move beyond surface-level conversations and embrace vulnerability, empathy, and intentionality, which brings about self-awareness and reflection. By being present in the moment, it creates this desire in me to seek what truly matters most in my life, which is deep meaningful connections.
—Tracey Abel, Assistant Director for Capital Construction & Engineering, Colorado State University

CONTENTS

FOREWORD

Mike Wood, MD, SASHE, CHC

There are moments in life when a single conversation can ignite change, inspire action, create unforeseen pivots, or heal wounds that have lingered for years. In today's world, where we're constantly connected yet often feel isolated, the art of meaningful dialogue is more important than ever. Kyle Majchrowski's second book, *Powerful Conversations Volume 2*, arrives at a time when our collective need for authentic connections, honest exchange, and transformative communication has never been greater.

Once upon a time...during an uneventful, peaceful breakfast in downtown Portland, Oregon, three healthcare project guys commiserated over the current state of their work. I use the term "healthcare guys" loosely. We were from diverse backgrounds with four things in common: 1) we had all come from the trades as teenagers; 2) we came to healthcare project management by default not by plan but via school project management, software implementation and clinical medicine; 3) we were all stymied by the lack of human dynamic intelligence within our chosen profession; and 4) we each wanted a decent breakfast.

I had two overwhelming thoughts as we progressed through the meal and ensuing passionate conversation that developed surrounding the lack of soft skills in our profession. The first is that "someone" needed to act. The second was that we were rapidly concluding that someone would be us. That conclusion was unnerving yet transformative. Fast forward a few days—mere days—and we had cooked up The Idea. We needed a location, participants, funding, and a meaningful agenda. Not just for a one-time conversation, but many to follow. A program, not a project.

Within a few more days, we had an agenda, place, date and time, participants committed to joining us, and funding (more or less). At our inaugural gathering, the hotel staff and local Fire Marshal informed us we had exceeded capacity. Gulp. We had discovered a gaping hole in communication and soft skills we had only sensed existed. For two days, Kyle, Scott, staff, and I scrambled to overcome the issue of overcrowding. It's hilarious how three massive introverts upstaged the Three Stooges, survived the chaos of our own making, and solved the opportunities of the moment. And yet...the Magic appeared to us and everyone who trusted us, believed in the greater good, and allowed us to stretch the boundaries of "Know yourself first, then know others."

Here we are today. Thousands of similar professionals have taken that leap of faith with us. It's humbling, almost embarrassing, to admit that a breakfast among three colleagues on a mission to positively affect the care of our Portland patients has become a national movement. I genuinely believe the movement has no boundaries except those people place upon themselves.

I watched, observed, coached, and mentored Kyle's work as it progressed and is expressed through his debut book, *Powerful Conversations*. I'm struck by his rare ability to blend warmth, candor, and actionable insight into every page. Now, with this second volume, Kyle dives deeper, building upon his foundational ideas and inviting us on a journey both personal and practical. Whether you're a leader striving to motivate your team, a friend hoping to support a loved one, or simply someone seeking deeper human connection, this book offers tools and wisdom that resonate at every level.

Kyle's approach is refreshingly honest. He doesn't shy away from the challenges that real conversations bring—the discomfort, vulnerability, and risk inherent in speaking our truth and truly listening to others. Through stories, strategies, and compassionate guidance, he illuminates how powerful conversations aren't just about words; they are about presence, intention, and the courage to be open. The stories in *Powerful Conversations* and *Powerful Conversations Volume 2* remind us that each exchange with our fellow humans has the potential to shape our lives and the lives of those around us.

As you turn these pages, you will discover practical frameworks and inspiring reflections that will empower you to build trust, resolve conflict, and foster genuine understanding. Kyle's voice is that of a wise companion—challenging us to reflect, offering us hope, and above all, inviting us to step into conversations that matter.

It's my sincere hope that *Powerful Conversations Volume 2* will not only inform you but also encourage you to engage more deeply and authentically with the world. Additionally, I strongly encourage you to embrace this message, make it a well-worn part of your library, and perhaps incorporate its ideas into your dialogue with colleagues. May this book serve as your guide to creating moments of connection, clarity, and transformation—one conversation at a time.

Congratulations to Kyle Majchrowski on this important work and mission. May its impact ripple far and wide, inspiring powerful conversations wherever its wisdom is shared.

CHAPTER 1

Conversations to Connections

TWENTY-FOUR HOURS BEFORE MY WIFE'S EARLY MORNING OUTPATIENT SURGERY, AN EMAIL POPPED UP WITH LAST-MINUTE REMINDERS.

Eat nothing after dinner, leave jewelry at home, arrive at 6:30 AM, and so on. On surgery day, our alarm sounded at 5 AM. The air was tense, and we got ready in silence, each of us knowing that being put under is never without risk. Our thirty-minute ride to the hospital was likewise quiet. No radio. We were both still groggy yet awake, preoccupied with what was coming. My own anxieties were rising. As the loving spouse with no firsthand experience of surgery, I could only guess what my wife was going through. I tried to be strong. Supportive. We parked close, grabbed our things, and headed inside.

Someone at check-in ticked off a list confirming identity, insurance, and payment. In the waiting area, someone else double-checked much of the same information and told us to wait for the care team to take my wife back to the prep area. She would need about 20 minutes to get ready, then I would be called back to sit in as multiple providers—nurses, anesthesiologist, surgeon—discussed the process, medications, expectations, and post-surgery care. At the end of that information dump, I was sent back to the waiting room. The surgeon would report to me after the procedure.

I settled in and sipped coffee. I reflexively pulled out my phone and laptop as if nonchalantly awaiting a flight. I aimed to bury myself in anything to take my mind off the surgery and all the things that could go wrong. I glanced at the morning news, checked email, and finally pulled out a book. I hoped my intentional distractions would keep me from feeling overwhelmed.

The surgeon eventually appeared and let me know everything went well. My wife did great. He said to expect her to be in recovery for about an hour, then left. A nurse called me in and walked me through discharge process: directions to the pharmacy for prescriptions, instructions for administering meds, warning signs to watch for at home, and how check out would work. Then I was sent back to the waiting room.

I picked up the prescriptions and waited a while longer before the staff informed me that I should get the car and meet my wife at the front door. I pulled up and went inside the foyer to wait. The staff wheeled out my wife, I helped her into my car, and we drove toward home.

I suddenly felt overcome. I hadn't grasped how much the ordeal stressed me out, and I wasn't the one who got knocked out and cut open.

I was a mix of tense, tired, and relief—a wreck, exhausted from all the pent-up emotions of the past few days and our experience of the past six hours. My feelings were buried deep inside, and while I expected I would need to toughen up to get through this day, the floodgates now opened.

Everything poured out. In the car. On the way home. Alone. Sort of. I grabbed my wife's hand as she nodded off in the passenger seat.

What dawned on me was that throughout the morning, in touch points with over a dozen staff at the hospital, no one—not one person—asked me "How are YOU doing?" I was never engaged as a person going through what people who have loved ones undergoing surgery go through.

Days later, my wife and I compared notes. The surgery was a success. The staff was highly competent. She was incredibly grateful. Yet we were treated as numbers, a statistic, another surgery to get done and processed through the system. The staff, while informative and nice, were like robots. They followed their scripts, smiled at appropriate moments, and executed their instructions. Perfectly. But not personally.

Never once did anyone see my wife or me as people. As individuals. As human beings. Healthcare? Perhaps. Human care? Not at all.

Why didn't people use this opportunity to ask my wife how she was doing? Why didn't anyone look at me and perceive that while I put on a brave face and would do anything for my wife, this entire ordeal was new, uncomfortable, anxious, and scary? Providers no doubt encounter emotions in patients and loved ones every day—does that make them numb to it? Are they coached to avoid talking to people as people? Are there legal limits? Do staff face such high productivity expectations that a personal conversation might add time and ding their numbers?

This occurrence isn't unique to surgery. Or healthcare. We experience disconnected interactions constantly. The people in our orbit are often just a means to obtaining something—delivering our order, educating our kid, scoring us a promotion and a raise.

Endless surface interactions make us lonely. Human beings crave deep, meaningful connections and relationships. We badly want them, yet as a society, we have devolved in how we create, develop, and nurture relationships. Our front porch conversations, exchanges at school events, and everyday communications are focused on give and take. I want something, we transact, and thus ends the interaction. Do we remember the person's name? It doesn't matter—unless we want to complain about them. Gone are the days of knowing the people in our lives—at school, the neighborhood, the gas station, or the coffee shop.

David Brooks, author of *The Second Mountain*, wrote, "We live in a culture of hyper-individualism. There is always tension between self and society, between the individual and the group. Over the past sixty years we have swung too far toward the self."

What is hyper-individualism? It's a heightened focus on personal goals, autonomy, and self-interest over the group or collective well-being. We celebrate individual wins, success, power, money, and freedom.

Isn't that a description of the American Dream? We emphasize personal goals, self-perception, and individual satisfaction at the expense of social connections and collective responsibility. You too can be rich, powerful, and successful. There is no team, only I. Sure, people exist who can help you become successful, but those people aren't as important as you.

What's wrong with this approach? Hyper-individualism sounds good. Focus on you, do your thing, and become successful. Yet a dark side has emerged. With sixty-plus years of living together yet apart in this way, our world is facing the consequences. A decline in community comes with decreasing trust, smaller social networks, and sinking engagement in anything outside of work.

Loneliness and mental health struggles are at all-time highs. Dr. Vivek Murthy, former Surgeon General of the United States, declared that the country continues to suffer from a loneliness epidemic. In 2023, the World Health Organization identified loneliness as a pressing global public health concern. Isolation is rampant with an ever-increasing number of people feeling disconnected, anxious, and depressed. Social isolation and loneliness are often considered individual struggles, though the WHO report shows the impact on communities and societies.

Apathy is also at an all-time high. What used to catalyze a nation, state, city, or community to come together now divides. Societal problems, environmental causes, and political challenges are dismissed unless an individual feels their direct impact on their success, finances, or well-being.

And we continue to feed this belief system. Books and social media posts recognize this "It's all about me" attitude and amplify it. You don't like what someone thinks of you? No problem—ignore them. Got feedback about your clothes? Don't give it a second thought. Been told your life choices are wrong? Tell 'em you're just being your authentic self. By encouraging people to ignore others because you and you alone are what matters, we pander to hyper-individualism.

These are very attractive solutions. They tell us what we want to hear. Yet they're nothing less than destructive and dangerous. Books, podcasts, posts—the advice caters to our personal needs with a clear message. Compassion and empathy steal your energy. Don't waste it on others—spend it on you. You are the most important person in the world, and anyone who challenges, contradicts, or conflicts with you in any way is simply wrong. Disregard their thoughts, disconnect from interactions, and discard the relationship.

This message is smashing the easy button to get through life. It's a shortcut with "be yourself" as the mantra that nobody else matters but you. No wonder it's popular. Who doesn't have days when they would prefer to do whatever they please while giving the world a giant middle finger?

This attitude makes for entertaining viral videos, clips, posts, and books, but we need to realize it has no substance. It doesn't do us any good in real life.

Take an executive who joins an established national firm and quickly realizes her style is vastly different from her peers. Behaving authentically lands her in human resources jail, facing complaints, frustrations, and directives to fit in. At 52 years old, Sandra is who she is— and clearly unwanted here. Hyper-individualism says she should simply walk away because others are all wrong and she is completely right.

This is an instance where the advice from meme-world can have disastrous consequences. Sandra likes the company. She's engaged in the work. She knows she has a distinctive approach and heard it was a primary attribute that got her hired. She shouldn't leave, nor should she conform. Sandra has an opportunity to grow her self-awareness, develop her intentionality, and bond. To build relationships. Strengthen connections. She isn't right. And the company isn't right. They all need to figure it out. Together.

In life, what matters is people, connection, and conversations. It's easy to lean back and tell off the world, and that jaded message indeed may feel good reverberating in your head, among your friends, and online. Yet for a long, purposeful, meaningful, impactful, and happy life, you can't simply claim "I'm me!" If you do, you'll soon find yourself alone, like too many people today, a casualty of hyper-individualism.

Hyper-individualism does even more damage in today's transactional culture. You want something from someone, you interact, get your thing, they get their thing, life goes on. No connection. No relationship. Is that bad? Not always. When I buy a coffee, I'm not interested in striking up a conversation beyond my order. Take my order, here's my money, give me my beverage of choice.

However, if I check into a hotel and the person behind the desk never puts down their phone and hands me the keys without talking to me, I feel ignored. Unseen. Often, I've just spent several hours alone—likely on an airplane—and I'm grateful when someone greets me and wishes me a good night's rest. I don't want a relationship. Just a brief and genuine momentary feeling of connection. I'm seen. I'm heard. I matter. And in a world where that person spends their day—or nights—behind a hotel desk serving hurried humans who perhaps are rude and condescending, maybe that person also needs a connection. To be seen. To be heard. To matter.

The world's drive to increase productivity has turned even fleeting interactions into technological transactions. From self-checkouts to ordering your meal through an app, we come face-to-face with people less and less. Even in settings that require talking to others, the vibe is transactional.

Has our hyper-individualized society made us unable to see others? Do we no longer know how to connect as humans?

It's true that transactions often make life easier. The exchange of value—information, money, or services—focuses on what we can get or give right now, in the short term, and surface-level interactions make everything faster. No vulnerability or trust necessarily.

These interactions, however, aren't enough to nourish us as people. We can't live without authentic connections.

We most likely picture "connecting" as something we reserve for people closest to us—for relationships that build over long periods of time where we can safely show vulnerability, empathy, and trust. We value what we get from connecting, including belonging, resilience, purpose, and comfort.

We know what genuine, deep connections feel like. We believe they are difficult to build and don't happen quickly. When we don't have them, we crave them. Once we have them, we want to hang onto them. When they are gone, we grieve our loss.

Many workplaces recognize how powerful connections can be among employees and have tried to bring them about through happy hours, small groups, and engagement trainings. Many of these experiences have the right goal in mind, but they have hit-or-miss outcomes.

How do we create connection? Genuine relationships? Interactions that turn us away from a focus on self and instead toward others?

Powerful Conversations.

My first book opened the door for Powerful Conversations, providing over 250 intentional questions within 21 topics to help people have meaningful conversations. They drive connection. They focus on both yourself and others. They put the conversation model into action: Connect, Think, Apply, Reach.

This model applies to the 21 topics in the book *Powerful Conversations* and to the 21 new topics in this book. As you read through each topic, have the conversation in your mind. Write down or journal your thoughts, feelings, and answers. Bring a friend to the conversation. Ask the questions of others. Bring a group together.

From individuals to small groups to book clubs to large organization leadership teams, these conversations have made and continue to make a difference in how we live and work.

David Brooks continued, "The only way out is to rebalance, to build a culture that steers people toward relation, community, and commitment—the things we more deeply yearn for, yet undermine with our hyper-individualistic way of life."

Get out there. Build a relationship, make a connection,
enter a community. Start the conversation today.

CHAPTER 2

Character

WHEN BEHAVIOR CONFLICTS WITH THE EXPECTATIONS OF OTHERS AND BOTH ALTERNATIVES ARE ARGUABLY RIGHT, CHARACTER IS THRUST TO THE FOREFRONT.

The team faced a serious dilemma. Early in their formation, its leaders bonded over behaviors and attributes all would abide by, including a rule that no one would remain in the office past 5 PM each day. The rule worked well for as long as the team included only the leaders who stepped up to this commitment. Each night by 5 PM, everyone was out the door. Then the team added associates and managers, greatly expanding the size of the group. One manager made clear he couldn't go along with the 5 PM cutoff. Leaving work at 5 PM would land him in peak traffic, quadrupling his commute time to almost two hours each evening. By staying until 6:30 PM, he could cut his drive to 30 minutes. This manager announced his decision and wouldn't budge.

The leaders pondered what to do. The rule was clear. Equally clear was the rule's intent in furthering work–life balance, and no one could argue that less time in the car is obviously positive. The upshot was that a situation now existed where two "right" decisions created a defining moment of character.

Defining moments emerge when we're faced with decisions that connect our personal identity to life in the real world. These moments not only define character but also build it. Each of the two right options presents a reasonable, thoughtful, and heartfelt choice. The challenge isn't good versus bad but right versus right.

Picture a work challenge requiring overtime for weeks on end. How do those long hours impact families and other essential relationships? While it's good to pull together and tackle the work for the good of the company, time with kids is equally important. Except that not everyone has kids. Those without children might get "volunteered" by others to shoulder the extra work. Tensions rise, conflict ensues, and a defining moment is created.

Consider a woman of color who was invited to join an interview panel for a position she has little to do with. The woman realizes the experience could further develop her skills as an interviewer and expand her knowledge outside her usual responsibilities. But she knows that the other interviewers are white men, and she recognizes her presence on the panel checks a diversity box. Her attendance will help the organization showcase its commitment to including different perspectives in the hiring process. But she doesn't want to be the "token minority woman."

It's a character-defining moment.

Dictionary.com defines character as "the aggregate of features and traits that form the individual nature of some person or thing." The Britannica Dictionary says character is "the way someone thinks, feels, and behaves." Collins dictionary adds, "The character of a person or place consists of all the qualities they have that make them distinct from other people or places."

Character can be articulated as the combination of your beliefs, ethics, values, experiences, and how those together show up in your life. This combination propels you to be a good person. You don't walk around randomly hitting people because your character tells you not to. You show up to work on time, give people the benefit of the doubt, and exchange money for goods and services instead of stealing—habits that showcase the character formed in you through many years and countless choices.

You may also believe that people shouldn't suffer alone because we're all in this together. And we should obey laws. Being kind is the right thing to do, even when the other person is a jerk. In a fight between good and evil, good should win. Wars are bad unless they're against evil countries. Holding these notions as principles comes from a core of beliefs and values that contribute to your character.

The complex combination of values, beliefs, and practical ethics defines your character. And there's one more very important piece. When you find yourself in defining moments, your character shows up in your decision-making.

THINK AND DISCUSS (PART ONE)

- What's your definition of character?
- Can you define your own character?
- How did you learn and develop your definition of character?
- What defining moments have you faced?

The development of character follows a meandering yet predictable path.

In *The Road to Character*, author David Brooks profiles people throughout history and the paths that created their character. Some subjects are famous and others relatively obscure. Each of their stories followed a similar arc. At some point in life, each person depicted actively chased the goals of money, success, fortune, and fame—maybe not all four, but at least one and often more.

Brooks considers this stage the beginning of character building, what he calls "Adam 1." This logical, thoughtful, action-oriented self knows that input leads to output, practice makes perfect, and hard work will be rewarded. We aren't born with character—we develop it over time. Many of us start with Adam 1 leading the way, aiming to get things done and impress the world.

As life progresses, our values solidify and our ethics form. For many people, there's a distinct turning moment when we truly own these values and ethics. Even as Adam 1 is winning at life—promoted, making money, and finding success—Adam 2 stirs inside us. Adam 2 is the voice in our heads and hearts of moral logic as opposed to economic logic. It encourages us to seek a greater good in order to gain strength within ourselves. This part of us begins to understand that humility and learning are our greatest success.

What does that really mean? That just as Adam 1 is attaining success, Adam 2 pops up and speaks the hard truth that so far in life we've been materialistic and power hungry, and because we've achieved everything, we therefore lack true character. Is it time to go on a journey to truly define our values, beliefs, and ethics? To build real character?

Sort of. But not quite! Recall the woman who was asked to be on the interview panel, who happened to be a middle manager in her mid-thirties. She hadn't achieved great power and strength, the pinnacle of Adam 1. And at that point in her life, she already possessed a strong sense of personal values, beliefs, and ethics, a sure sign of Adam 2. Here's the nuance: Adam 1 and Adam 2 aren't linear. Adam 1 doesn't happen before 2. As life happens, both Adams coexist within us. What matters is which Adam is louder, which one we heed, and the degree to which the attributes of Adam 2 have solidified.

That's what creates and defines our character at any given moment. If we reflect on this dynamic, we can see the push and pull of character formation happening within us.

Mollie Roth is the founder and chair of the Arrowhead Translational Microbiome Conference, a convener of leading microbiome individuals and organizations. Her passion for the field ignited as she read one article, then another, and she insatiably consumed anything she could find on the subject. Soon, she was creating a conference. Why would anyone do such a thing?

Mollie was raised by a mom who instilled in her that she is strong and that she can do anything. As long as Mollie can remember, her mom created confidence, strength, and power in her that she could accomplish whatever she wanted to. She is a go-getter, a perpetual mold-breaker, a leader who stands out not because she chases accolades or awards but instead does everything with heart, energy, and passion. She was a successful attorney in New York City who was recognized, rewarded financially, and living high— until she realized she despised what her life had become. For six years, she managed to convince herself she was doing the right thing and living her best life. But she was kidding herself. Something was missing. Her work wasn't aligned with who she really was.

Mollie observes that many men are locked into pursuing an upward career trajectory as the only measure of success, and many women take any job necessary to support their kids. People become hyper-focused on their families and themselves and therefore rarely engage in bigger causes outside themselves, whether charities or the needs of neighbors.

To Mollie, it's essential that we combine doing what needs to be done to support our inner circle with engaging in larger causes. It's simply what we're supposed to do.

Mollie doesn't have a discrete list of values or principles she aims to live by, but she always sensed what matters to her and consciously endeavors to stay true to herself. For example, although she lacked a strong relationship with her dad, she cared for him before his passing because that's the person she wants to be. She created the microbiome conference out of seemingly nowhere as she recognized a need, felt pulled to it, and knew it was the right thing to do.

Mollie doesn't point to a single character-defining moment, having always felt she could do anything. Her success is rooted in her upbringing, followed by the always-present and always-clarifying combination of values, ethics, and beliefs that articulate her character.

Although Mollie's Adam 2 has always been a strong voice throughout her life, at times that voice announced itself with more definition, power, and influence. The same is true for most leaders in politics, business, and community groups. Those with strong Adam 2s show up when under pressure, stand in the face of opposition, present with steadfastness, and are firm when it matters. On the other hand, we're quick to notice when people's character seems hypocritical, like when they say one thing and do another. Or their positions flip-flop, with their values, beliefs, and ethics changing depending on the situation. These character shortcomings make them difficult to trust or follow.

Martha was a leader nearing the end of her career who saw an opportunity to create something more with her teams. She focused on personal connection and began holding monthly gatherings intended to help people grow deeper together as human beings. This effort was soon undermined by her own contradictory actions.

As these gatherings were taking off, Martha's direct reports were struggling to work with others in the organization. It would seem obvious for this older and wiser Martha to resolve those conflicts by leaning into deeper connections. However, her years of work had formed strong habits, and her beliefs, ethics, and values weren't going to change overnight just because she discovered people had a need to connect. She did what she knew best, rallying her direct reports and complaining mightily to other leaders about the difficulty of working with their people. Instead of encouraging her team to strengthen connections and break through the conflicts, she fell back into well-worn patterns of going on the attack and compelling others to change.

Martha is another in a long line of people where their environment and personal unwillingness to lean into their Adam 2 resulted in a demonstrated lack of character.

How can we be more like Mollie and less like Martha? Start by taking time to reflect, think, and intentionally craft the six elements of character in yourself:

1. **Self-awareness.** Understand how your strengths, opportunities, and motivations guide your actions and decision-making.
2. **Backstory.** Journal a detailed background story of yourself that explains your values, ethics, and beliefs.
3. **Ethical decision-making.** Examine what ethics influence your moral compass.
4. **Empathy and kindness.** Explore where you're most able to be kind and empathetic.
5. **Self-discipline.** Practice self-control and commitment.
6. **Positive relationships.** Surround yourself with people who encourage your growth and hold you to high standards.

THINK AND DISCUSS (PART TWO)

- Where have you seen failures of character?
- Which of the six elements of character comes naturally to you?
- Which elements are more challenging?
- How do you build your own character?

Character develops over time through an ongoing—and repeatable— process of defining your purpose and acting accordingly.

Character involves sacrifice for the sake of principle, sometimes at the cost of relationships, followers, support, money, fame, and power. Creating character doesn't happen without practice, time, and experience.

Joseph L. Badaracco of HBR describes an effective character development process in the real world of business. He writes, "Specifically, they (managers) are able to take time out from the chain of managerial tasks that consumes their time and undertake a process of probing self-inquiry—a process more often carried out on the run rather than in quiet seclusion. They dig below the busy surface of their daily lives and refocus on their core values and principles. Once uncovered, those values and principles renew their sense of purpose at work and act as a springboard for shrewd, pragmatic, politically astute action. By repeating this process again and again throughout their work lives, these executives craft an authentic and strong identity based on their own, rather than on someone else's, understanding of what is right. And in this way, they begin to make the transition from being a manager to becoming a leader."

Viewed through the lens of character development, every situation of life either defines or further refines our beliefs, ethics, and values. Each moment is an opportunity to put those into play, to stand behind them, to test if the character we're creating works in the moment and aligns with what we hold to be valuable and true.

THINK AND DISCUSS (PART THREE)

- Take a moment to schedule appointments with yourself over the next six months to regularly reflect on your character. Use the six elements as your guide.
- What upcoming defining moments do you foresee for yourself?
- How can you help others develop their character?
- What defining moments are others going through right now that you can lean into?

Building character often involves developing a
bold sense of personal integrity.

Sean was thrust into a team of strong, intelligent, and experienced coworkers with many successes and established norms. One pattern he immediately observed was multitasking during meetings. In one fluid motion, arriving attendees said hello, sat down, pulled out a laptop, and began responding to emails. This habit was justified as an outcome of everyone being so busy.

Sean understood the rationale, but the experience concerned him. He had been to many similar meetings where people half-listened and therefore made half-baked decisions. Sean saw how these actions caused interpersonal damage. Although he "knew his place" as the newest and one of the youngest team members, he also felt inwardly compelled to speak up.

Sean found a few supportive team members and indeed stepped forward. He let his own character lead the way.

Bill had delivered countless successes in his career and landed a position at a new organization. He was very comfortable discussing finances and quickly discovered his teammates preferred to avoid any kind of money talk. When a specific money challenge became evident in his own area, Bill knew the right thing to do was to lean into it, get it on the agenda, and lead an open discussion. His peers were ready to pounce. They knew that any negatives around money in Bill's area were opportunities to dismantle his team and build their own kingdoms. Bill anticipated this confrontation, and he was led by his Adam 2. For the good of his people and the organization, he acted with transparency, accountability, and vulnerability. He led with his steadfast beliefs, values, and ethics. He led with his character.

Character means practicing honesty, respecting others, taking responsibility for your actions, overcoming challenges, learning from mistakes, and demonstrating empathy—even when it's difficult. Essentially, it's doing the right thing even when it's hard and accepting accountability for your choices. While it's easy to criticize others when they appear to have a failure of character, the better path is focusing on your own Adam 2 and ensuring you live according to your own best self.

CHAPTER 3

___

Burnout

CHRONIC STRESS QUASHES OUR GREATEST HOPES AND HIGHEST DREAMS. AND WHO HASN'T BEEN THERE?

Jeff was beyond excited about starting his new job. After years of bouncing between roles, he felt like this was the one. He landed the position of contracts administrator, a dull-sounding title that, for Jeff, was his dream come true. He would finally get his chance to impact the world, working on a team of professionals to ensure adherence to policy, procedure, and most importantly, ethics. Many of his new teammates were lawyers, and together they would ensure fairness in university expenditures on goods and services. In a large and convoluted institution, it was where the rubber met the road.

Jeff's first few months involved typical onboarding with welcome trainings, accessing university systems, gaining software access, and learning the secret handshake. Then came focused training within his department—how to create requests for proposals, publish RFPs, select vendors, create and administer contracts, and terminate contracts when delivery went awry. For Jeff, these details made the job a great fit. He was naturally analytical, organized, and responsible, and he quickly got to work.

As his first year unfolded, Jeff found deep joy in his work. His teammates were excellent partners, fully recognizing his drive and passion. His role touched nearly every business unit within the university, and he began to work on longer and more complicated projects.

After Jeff's first year, the university faced financial strains. The ability of Jeff's group to support the purchase of goods and services diminished, and the budgets shrank further in his second year. His teammates told him not to worry. They had seen this before, and it was all cyclical. While a few newer people were reassigned or laid off, Jeff was safe enough and kept on. His workload temporarily lessened, then caught him off guard as it shot up. Way up. Instead of overseeing a handful of large projects, Jeff absorbed responsibility for dozens of small projects that had been handled by the people who were let go—each project with just as many steps, checklists, and deliverables as the larger ones. He found himself toiling late into the evenings and some weekends just to keep up.

Jeff had always taken pride in his health. When he started this job, he was getting up early to work out four days a week. He took time to shop for healthy foods, and most days he packed his own nutritious lunch. As year two ground on, his health began to suffer. He ate out, skipped lunches, and barely found enough time to sleep, much less wake up early to exercise. Work had now become what seemed to be the only thing on his mind, even invading his dreams several times a week. He was never able to let go of the work and truly rest. There was just too much to do, and the university counted on him getting his work done to achieve the mission. His teammates kept telling him to hang in there. After all, they said, times like this never last forever.

THINK AND DISCUSS (PART ONE)

- Where in your life do you experience ongoing stress?
- Have you ever sacrificed your own well-being for your job?
- When have you felt especially strained—emotionally, physically, or mentally?
- When have you noticed bad habits creeping and dominating your life? When have you seen that happen in others?

Burnout is a state of emotional, physical, and mental exhaustion caused by excessive and prolonged stress.

For months, Jeff powered through. He kept up with his work—barely—

and with frequent illness. He had hardly been sick a day in his life, though now he suffered frequent upset stomachs and headaches. He tried to take sick days here and there, although the amount of work and the availability of technology just meant he wound up working from home. Feeling ill pushed exercising further out of reach, and when he attempted to work out, his feeling out of shape just made him depressed. He hadn't made his own lunch for months; instead, he grabbed junk food from vending machines or ordered fast food and ate without leaving his desk.

Jeff began to wonder if he was cut out for the job. Did he pursue the wrong role? Was he kidding himself that he could do the work, especially keeping up with a team full of smart lawyers? Was he tough enough to get through this? Maybe he wasn't as good as he thought. Maybe he shouldn't be here. The thought of another job search was more than he could handle. More work loomed each day, and there wasn't enough time even to breathe.

After many months, Jeff's situation at the university didn't improve. The workload was impossible, open positions in his group remained in a hiring freeze and unfilled, and Jeff was a mess. Long gone were the days of big wins and applause for him and his team. Jeff's leader was equally spent, and he had stopped expressing gratitude to the team. The entire team was in a daze, seeming to simply get through each day. Jeff's energy, drive, and passion were a distant memory. He slogged through each day just trying to survive. His attitude had soured, he had no personal time outside work, and each day was at best a chore. Even getting out of bed became a massive effort. And reaching out for help? Jeff didn't see anyone else asking for help or support, and besides, just the thought of saying something brought up feelings of shame within him.

Making things worse, Jeff's teammates noticed his work was going downhill. He no longer had the capacity to care, and his productivity plummeted. When others offered support, Jeff seemed cold and distant. He found daily opportunities to badmouth everything about the situation, and others within the university agreed with his perception. His cynicism was shared by many of his colleagues, who were suffering just as much as he was.

Burnout occurs when a person feels overwhelmed, emotionally drained, and unable to meet constant demands. The World Health Organization (WHO) is clear that burnout is not a medical condition. Burnout differs from stress and depression. Instead, burnout is an occupational situation.

According to the National Institutes of Health,

The term "burnout" was coined in the 1970s by the American psychologist Herbert Freudenberger. He used it to describe the consequences of severe stress and high ideals in caregiving professions. Doctors and nurses, for example, who sacrifice themselves for others, would often end up being "burned out"— exhausted, listless, and overwhelmed. Nowadays, the term is not only used for these caregiving professions, or for the dark side of self-sacrifice. It can affect anyone, from stressed-out career-driven people and celebrities to overworked employees and homemakers.

There are three generally accepted components of burnout:

1. **Exhaustion:** People feel drained emotionally and physically. They lack energy, resulting in feeling tired and overwhelmed. Physical symptoms can include stomach issues.
2. **Alienation and depersonalization:** People experiencing burnout lack connection to their work. Their feelings of stress and frustration lead to cynicism about their work, environment, and colleagues. They shut down emotionally, withdraw, and distance themselves from others.
3. **Decreased sense of accomplishment and reduced performance:** Burnout impacts productivity at work and at home. People can become broadly negative, have difficulty concentrating, and lack ambition.

When the technology sector collapsed following the events of 9/11, my little startup technology company folded. After two years of running the business I started, I wasn't sure what to do next. Although some people would see the closure as an opportunity to reinvent, I felt crushed. I had poured two years of my life into a software company that dissolved in the blink of an eye. Part of me died—a big part!

Two years of constant stress isolated me and left me with no time for a personal life. And now, with nothing to show for it, I shut down. When my brother came to visit, we went for a jog, and as I panted through the miles, he suggested I apply at Home Depot. Given the economic downturn, that may not be a stupid choice. But his words went straight to my heart. I was burned out, sliding into depression, and that comment felt like it devalued every- thing I had accomplished so far. It pushed me over the edge.

THINK AND DISCUSS (PART TWO)

- Where have you observed people suffering from burnout?
- What job stressors contributed to their decline? How did they behave toward work and their coworkers?
- What additional environmental factors influenced their burnout?
- Which of the three components of burnout did they exhibit?

Understanding burnout as a workplace state helps us reframe our experiences as a response to an external situation. Digging deeper into the condition and its causes helps us envision potential solutions.

Jeff experienced all three aspects of burnout. He was clearly exhausted, barely slept, ate poorly, and never moved his body. He struggled to make it through each day, and he couldn't shake his frequent illnesses. His verbal outbursts and ongoing criticisms of department leadership and the university evidenced distrust toward his employer to the point where some thought he was past the point of no return. None of this happened overnight. The three aspects slowly built over a period longer than two years. Burnout does not happen in an instant; instead, burnout is a long-term chronic issue.

Had Jeff's environment changed for the better—less work and more gratitude—his attitude might have perked up for a moment. But it was a strong possibility that an external change wouldn't temper his cynicism. His work continued to decline, with missed deadlines, sloppy product, and a loss of all-important customer focus.

Have you ever been in this state? When your health took a hit, you felt impacted physically, disconnected, and nothing you did seemed to matter? And you wondered how in the world you got here?

During a period of my career when I built custom homes, some truly nice people asked me to investigate a built-in vacuum system. On my drive to a business that designed and installed these systems, I broke down, so overwhelmed by emotion that I had to pull over. Overcome by emotion, I got angry, cried, yelled, and screamed as I sat in my truck feeling like a complete failure. What was I doing with my life? How had my focus devolved to dealing with luxury vacuum systems? This wasn't an opportunity to learn something new. It was pure embarrassment. The task felt like it defined me as a person, and it crushed me. I wanted to do something meaningful with my life, and this surely wasn't it. I plotted how I could quit. I was done.

Researcher Christina Maslach, PhD, emeritus professor of psychology at the University of California, Berkley, explains that burnout results from difficulties in any of six core areas:

1. **Workload:** What are you juggling? Do you have too much to do with too little time, tools, or information to get it done?
2. **Control:** Do you have control over what you do and how you do it? Are you able to improve work processes, innovate, and be creative in completing tasks?
3. **Reward:** Are you paid fairly? Do you receive good benefits? How is your contribution recognized?
4. **Workplace Community:** Who do you connect with regularly—coworkers, leader, customers, support people? Are people supportive of solving problems, accomplishing work, and pitching in? Or are they toxic and combative—seen in turf wars, silos, and defensiveness?
5. **Fairness:** Are you treated fairly? Does the system uphold ethical principles—or does it empower liars, cheaters, and thieves? Do politics dominate your day to the point where you feel you're constantly losing?
6. **Values:** Are your personal values aligned with your work and the organization? Are you asked to do things that conflict with your values?

While volume of work is the problem most people associate with burnout, the response can be brought on by any of these six factors. Dr. Maslach's research reveals that many organizations deal with burnout using a wellness approach where a manager or HR representative suggests the sufferer should see a therapist. Remember, the WHO stated clearly that burnout is not a medical condition. Then what exactly is it?

Burnout is a situation directly caused by your workplace. Each of the six elements Dr. Maslach identifies is within the organization's realm of influence. The first three are tactical. Straightforward. With the right resources, workload can and should be managed. Working people until they drop is unethical, and only extreme situations briefly call for chronic workload mismanagement. Moreover, the top-down leader-knows-all management styles of the past are just that—in the past. Today's workforce thrives on empowerment, innovation, and control over how and where they spend their time. Compensating people fairly for their work is paramount.

The other three elements are more complicated, and solutions aren't always clear. Creating a sense of workplace community requires leaders to embrace their responsibility to intentionally create and drive a culture where relationships are recognized as a value-add rather than a nice-to-have. Part of that effort is leaders striving to keep politics to a minimum and hold liars and cheats accountable. Employees who are good producers whose methods nevertheless damage the culture must be removed. While posting values in the breakroom or flashing them on a screensaver is quaint, how do employees see those values in action—and upheld every day? How do accountability and recognition align with the organization's stated principles?

In any setting where factions are at odds with each other, statements like "It's not in my budget," "You pay for that," "I don't have the people to help you," and "That group did something bad" all feel like normal parts of the workday. It's natural to protect your people while pointing fingers. But "natural" doesn't make bad behaviors acceptable. Do leaders confront these issues, ignore them, or overlook them in favor of short-term gains of getting things done?

Leaders are more responsible for burnout than any employee, because they create and control the environments that directly contribute to all six elements of burnout. The good news? With intention, all six can be overcome.

THINK AND DISCUSS (PART THREE)

- How do you know if people around you are suffering from burnout?
- What can you do to better recognize the symptoms of burnout?
- Does it feel safe to talk about burnout in your workplace? Why—or why not?
- How can you help others prevent their own burnout?

When our bodies, minds, and hearts are pushed to the brink for extended periods of time, our human defenses show up.

After nearly three years on the job, Jeff woke up, went to work, packed his stuff, and walked out. He took two weeks to just be still. Then he began to reflect and understand how the past three years went for him. The pause gave him space to realize he had become someone he never wanted to be. He saw a spark inside himself that reignited when he got out of his work environment. While researching and understanding his own burnout, he started eating better and exercising. He began to see why the environment and culture of his former workplace caused burnout. And he began searching for a job in an organization where leaders took the six elements of burnout seriously and endeavored each day to prevent them—for the sake of the company, for the sake of employees, for their own sake.

Many people feel like quitting isn't an option. They need the job to keep up with the mortgage, bills, kids' needs, and more. They don't have time to look for another job. Those feelings are completely understandable. But the long-term consequences of staying in a burnout-inducing situation can't be ignored.

Burnout is a human response to stressors. Our bodies push back. While we may mentally convince ourselves to toughen up, suck it up, and drive through it, our subconscious knows better. Eventually, our bodies tell our physical selves to knock it off, recognize enough is enough, and make plans to exit the situation. Since burnout isn't a medical diagnosis, it takes self-awareness, awareness of your environment, and awareness of those around you to get ahead of burnout before it has severe consequences. Burnout may drive you to quit in a time and manner where you have little control, develop chronic disease such as hypertension or heart disease, or worse. Think hard about how you can choose to proactively seek a healthier setting on your own terms—so you can thrive!

CHAPTER 4

Ego and Power

BEST-SELLING AUTHOR RYAN HOLLIDAY STATES, "WHEREVER YOU ARE, WHATEVER YOU'RE DOING, YOUR WORST ENEMY ALREADY LIVES INSIDE YOU: YOUR EGO."

He continues, "It's that petulant child inside every person, the one that chooses getting his or her way over anything or anyone else. It's the sense of superiority and certainty that exceeds the bounds of confidence and talent. It's when the notion of ourselves and the world grows so inflated that it begins to distort the reality that surrounds us."

We want to be recognized and acknowledged for the good we do—for who we are. Ego is always present, telling us we're not only good but great—and nothing can stop us. We know what we're doing. We're worth listening to. We have the title, the position, and the answers. Our ego builds us up to greatness.

Ego in sports is obvious. Take the infamous Allen Iverson rant. He was supposed to be the next Michael Jordan when he joined the 76ers as a rookie in the NBA in 1997. In 2002, the 76ers lost in Game 5 by 43 points, an embarrassing way to end the season. In a media interview a few days later, he exploded with bombast that felt extreme even by professional basketball standards. Iverson believed he was so good, so talented, so confident that practice was irrelevant. Games were all that mattered. When asked about the team, he responded, "How the hell can I make my teammates better by practicing?"

Or there's Kanye West. Charlie Sheen. Jake Paul. James Corden. Search online for "celebrities with egos" and you find an overload of content from articles to Reddit boards to videos. It turns out that celebrities driven by ego who behave badly gain large audiences.

We all recognize that people with large egos are full of themselves. We might still fall for the fallacy that they can do no wrong—or we at least let them slide without answering for their missteps. Power, fame, and fortune grant the egotistical near-limitless freedom to do and say whatever they want. Allen Iverson skipped practice. Kanye West felt free to interrupt another artist's acceptance speech. James Corban reportedly doesn't feel a need to treat people well because he puts himself above them.

What about non-celebrities? The workplace is often where ordinary people give their ego a free rein. Take David, a middle manager tasked with implementing a company-wide effort of consolidation, purchasing power, market leverage, cost reduction, and standardization of processes and deliverables—a load of business jargon for "use our power and size to get the best deal from our vendors." David saw a path forward and ran full speed ahead.

David did his own job and everyone else's, writing the request for proposal and making selections singlehandedly. He proclaimed himself the company's technical authority, at times even calling himself the sole expert in his field.

No one was surprised when David rolled out his changes, and they weren't received well. He shifted tactics and took his ego on the road, telling people in the field his reasons for the changes, why he was right, and pointing to data that supported his effort. He envisioned himself as the champion, cheerleader, instructor, and savior, bringing light to darkness.

David met resistance everywhere he went. Although his ego took a hit, he kept on ticking. He told himself what doesn't kill you only makes you stronger. He circled back to resistors, admitting things weren't handled well and the whole thing was rushed—but asserting he was still right. He knew where the business needed to go, and his path was the only way forward.

As David continued to project his point of view, many questioned his authenticity. Sure, he had a good personality and was generally liked. But his ego kept shining through. Like when he claimed he was so smart that only he could see the entire industry was broken.

THINK AND DISCUSS (PART ONE)

- Who comes to mind when you think of people who have big egos?
- What notable characteristics do these people display?
- How do they behave toward people?
- Do their actions and behaviors help them succeed—or not? Explain.

Ego is often tied to past trauma. Trauma can contribute to people seeking attention, affirmation, and recognition because of an experience where they felt powerless or defenseless.

The possible traumatic origin of an inflated ego might come as a surprise. The more commonly understood cause of having an ego is also real. People develop large egos when they begin to see themselves as infallible, perhaps the result of hanging on to the attention they have received over the years. Let's face it. Many work cultures encourage, recognize, and reward egotistical behavior, without explicitly stating this, therefore creating an ego/reward cycle that reinforces egotistical behavior.

Why would any company reward egos? Ego and success often are symbiotic, with one reinforcing the other. Results drive success, success brings praise, and praise reinforces ego. Few people like the behaviors associated with large egos, but in a moment of crisis, a leader's confidence and charisma can overshadow or outweigh the presence of ego.

Take Angie, a leader brought in to rescue clothing stores in three cities. She was the fifth leader in six years, and many employees scoffed at her arrival, saying openly she was just the next in the revolving door of leaders. Angie, however, knew the industry and brought a level of perceived humility most employees saw as positive. She was kind, asked questions, and forthrightly stated that she came to fix things. Nevertheless, throughout the first year, people kept their distance. In the meantime, Angie made small gains with her business unit, which won her modest recognition from the parent company.

Then opportunity struck. A competitor was struggling, and Angie saw an opening to initiate a takeover. She jumped on the task. While she had help available within her company, the potential expansion was her chance to make her mark, so she chose to work alone. She knew the acquisition would take time, and she led her employees along by saying that fixing her previous company had taken a long time and a lot of effort, and asking them to be patient as she labored behind the scenes.

For months, Angie worked on the acquisition under the radar, and once the process hit the point of no return, she announced her plans, leaving her own company no choice but to pursue the deal. Angie was so confident and had made many promises on behalf of her company that she put the company in the position of overpaying for the struggling competitor. All that mattered to Angie was the recognition she would receive from the expansion.

Company leaders dug into the proposed deal to determine if it made sense. In the meetings that followed, Angie knew all the right things to say. She flattered and schmoozed the decision makers. She attacked the critics who asked questions and sought a better deal. She was so confident in the agreement that she attacked the character of opponents, sniped at data analysis, and fudged figures to make the deal look better than it was. The voice of ego in her head was so loud that she leveraged all her power and then some to get the deal done, bulldozing anyone who could possibly get in her way.

Stanford professor Dr. Jeffrey Pfeffer asserts that seeking workplace power allows us to live longer and healthier lives, can create wealth, and get things done. He says that the world isn't fair, and therefore, performance alone won't get us power. We must play politics and be savvy in workplace culture to win. In his book 7 Rules of Power, he offers the following practices to get things done and advance your career:

1. **Get out of your own way:** He says, "The combination of motivated cognition and people's generally poor ability to discern deceit means that inauthentic behavior is unlikely to be uncovered." In other words, don't believe all the moral and ethics stuff you've learned. If you want power, let go of altruistic beliefs and behaviors.

2. **Break the rules:** Since the rules tend to favor those already strong in power, it's easier to ask forgiveness than permission.

3. **Appear powerful:** Anger and attack are more powerful than sadness and remorse. When questioned, get angry.

4. **Build a powerful brand:** Develop your story and stand out by being appropriately controversial.

5. **Network Relentlessly:** Spend time interacting with useful people—emphasis on useful.

6. **Use your power:** Bring in supporters and move out opponents. Get rid

of people not on your side.

7. **Success excuses almost everything:** Victors write their own history, and they rewrite the history of others. This last rule is the most important of all.

It feels obvious these "rules" are egotistical in nature. However, Dr. Pfeffer provides compelling evidence that using these behaviors indeed helps people obtain power. He neither endorses nor rejects these rules—he simply states that if you want power, his research shows that these rules are what people enact to achieve great amounts of power.

Angie followed many of these rules as she pushed the acquisition to closure. The result? The company recognized her. The takeover was approved by top leaders, albeit reluctantly by some. Angie took a victory lap. She made sure everyone knew what she and she alone had accomplished, reminded them constantly how great the combined company would be, and even took credit for things she had nothing to do with, just because it bolstered her power. As Rule 1 says, get out of your own way. If you feel that lying, exaggerating, or cheating is a problem, then realize you won't gain power. Angie lied—repeatedly—but as Rule 7 states, once you have power, your lies and bad behavior will be forgiven.

Is this scenario a problem? Ego seems to let bias and selfishness run unchecked. We believe so strongly that we're right—and everyone else is wrong—that our self-absorption prevents us from seeing the world through a rational lens.

The question we must ask ourselves is this: Should we intentionally seek to manage our own egos—or not?

THINK AND DISCUSS (PART TWO)

- Think of a time when you got "stuck in your head," convinced you were right and everyone else was wrong. What were the circumstances?
- Are confidence and ego different? In what ways?
- Do you agree with Dr. Pfeffer's rules? Why—or why not?
- Has embracing your ego helped you succeed? When and where?

While some companies prioritize idealistic virtues that strive to prevent egocentric behaviors, those companies are rare.

If you think that Angie's story is unique, guess again. There are Angies in every company in the world, and Angies are regularly recognized and rewarded. They grab power to achieve results, and the outcomes they achieve further reinforce their power.

But what drives people like Angie and David? Does their motivation come from a good place? Is it a need for attention? To prove to everyone how smart they are? Do we want to reward egotism with greater influence and wealth? Or should we just accept that the end justifies the means?

Angie and David both dismissed people who challenged them along the way. Although they used words like "transparency" and "honesty" and expressed a desire for feedback, in reality, they ignored critiques and charged forward. They flattered others and leveraged networking to check boxes, knowing they were too smart for others to see what they were really doing. They believed they were always the smartest person in the room. They assumed they understood everyone's perceptions, excuses, and comfort level, and Angie and David had arrived on scene to show everyone "the" way.

The frustrating part? People like David and Angie often get the short-term win along with recognition and rewards, then leave the company for a more lucrative opportunity. What's wrong with that? If you were Angie or David, what's wrong with achieving something and then getting compensated for that achievement? In both cases, Angie and David left extreme damage in the aftermath of their "successes."

Angie and David would still argue today that they did great things. Their personal versions of how events went down are embellished, exaggerated versions that their egos have long repeated in their heads. As Ryan Holiday states, ego is about being "stuck in our heads instead of participating in the world around us." And the ego reinforces our belief system that our version of reality is the one true version.

THINK AND DISCUSS (PART THREE)

- How do other people's egos impact the people around them?
- How can you help others recognize their ego?

- How can you help others see the impact their ego has on others?
- How do you recognize when egos are in play, and how can you help prevent the damage that egotistical behavior creates?

Is ego all bad? That depends. It's up to us to decide if and how our egos determine our paths.

Betterhelp.com states, "The focus of humanistic psychology may be an individual's subjective experience and the journey toward self-actualization, which is typically defined as the process of realizing your full potential as a human being. Humanistic psychologists normally believe that the ego is a crucial aspect of the self, as it can mediate between the individual's inner desires and the outside world's demands. The ego can be seen as a tool for self-expression and self-discovery, and it may play a vital role in helping individuals fulfill their potential and achieve a sense of self-actualization."

Dr. Pfeffer makes a strong case from his lifetime of work on power that the world rewards bad behavior related to ego with power, success, and wealth. The challenge we all face is recognizing our own egos and asking if the choices we make for ourselves and others are truly good—or if we're acting solely to satisfy our own ego and ignoring the harmful impacts on others. Do we want to do life knowing that we lied, cheated, and stole to get power?

And once we have power, what do we do? Elon Musk, the richest man in the world, broke rules and treated people badly, making him widely recognized as a jerk. Is he now using his power for good? Nike founder Phil Knight, who made millions using kids in sweatshops to make his products, donates millions to charity. Does that make up for abusing children? Jeff Bezos created Amazon with a goal to get you to buy things when you want to buy them, not necessarily when you need them. Is Jeff Bezos using his power and wealth for good?

We each have choices to make. Do we care if we see ourselves objectively? Do we want to be an example to others? Does it matter if we positively impact the world? Or do we want to settle for something less?

CHAPTER 5

———

Anxiety

AS LONG AS LIFE BRINGS TROUBLES—REAL AND IMAGINED—ANXIETY WILL BE THERE. HARDLY ANYONE COMPLETELY ESCAPES WORRY, AND ALMOST EVERYONE FINDS IT DIFFICULT TO SHAKE.

Consider these three varied experiences of anxiety.

Ethan

Throughout all four years of high school, my oldest son ran cross country. From his first 5k—a painful 33 minutes in worn-out shoes—to breaking 20 minutes his senior year at an early winter Turkey Trot, nearly every race day hit the same way. Ethan would wake up and begin what he called "getting into his head." His mind spun up like a flywheel, and as hours passed, his doubts revved faster. By meet time, his flywheel was whirling near maximum speed, and his mind was filled with worry and apprehension. All his training and preparation weren't enough to slow his internal expectations and the resulting stresses that spun inside him. Outwardly, he appeared focused, deep in mental preparation. Inwardly, he was consumed by self-doubt. He went to a dark place.

Tom

Tom's 20 years as a leader were filled with kudos and recognition, often the highest marks possible for effectiveness and impact. He was personable, friendly, kind, and family-oriented, a man known for caring deeply about his team and company. His work in a highly regulated industry meant that adherence to policy, documentation, and procedure was essential to keeping the business running.

Tom began one morning engaged in his typical duties, meeting with folks to jumpstart the day, when a leader from corporate showed up unannounced. Tom never had an issue with these visits, even if they were a surprise. He took pride in how he ran the place and looked forward to showing people from the larger organization how well things functioned. This visit felt different. After Tom got people up and running, he was working through emails. Lynn barged into his office. He had an open-door policy, although most people knocked and politely asked if he had a moment. Lynn pointed a finger at him and said she had proof he hadn't been doing one of his duties. Tom was so taken aback that he was stunned silent. Lynn stared at him intently and demanded to see his work logs. As soon as Tom produced his paper records, Lynn snatched them and abruptly left. Tom sat alone in shock, questioning what had just happened and why.

Jill

Jill led her high-functioning unit firmly yet fairly, and the team had great respect for her. Her leadership made all the difference to the group's tight bonds. They shared group chats outside work, regularly hung out for a drink, and did non-work activities on weekends. She was unquestionably the leader, and yet they truly were all friends.

When Jill returned to work after a vacation, her team asked about her travels. She shared stories about her unusual destination. When her team asked what was most different about the place, she repeated some slang and "local speak" she said was shocking. Her team—her friends—were surprised by her experiences. One had traveled to the same place and agreed that the cultural differences were startling. Everyone chimed in during the exchange except Byron, the newest team member, who stayed silent.

THINK AND DISCUSS (PART ONE)

1. When have you felt anxious? What circumstances prompted your anxiety?
2. What makes you anxious today?
3. What parts of your day and life do you feel are in your control?
4. What things do you feel are out of your control?

When anxiety gets a foothold in our minds, it can rapidly take over. How we react to these pressures is deeply personal.

Ethan

Ethan approached each race the same way. Practices went consistently well, his teammates recognized him as a leader, and he almost always looked forward to the next run. He sailed through his junior year, living in the sweet spot of no pressure to be the team's top runner yet enjoying a constant stream of better times. With no job to worry about, school under control, and dating happening but not seriously, there was little on his mind besides being in the moment and anticipating faster and faster runs. He still felt the flywheel, but for the moment, his anxiety was manageable. It spun up the morning of each race day without overwhelming him.

Tom

A few hours passed after Lynn walked out with his record book. Tom remained puzzled. He did his best to remain calm and do his job, yet he couldn't help but wonder what he could have done wrong. In the absence of information, Tom made things up. He wasn't sure what to do next, and before he could decide, Lynn returned. She wanted Tom to pull video security footage. Tom was shocked. He asked Lynn if she thought he was lying. She didn't respond. She just continued her demands for the recordings.

Tom went from confused to defensive to panicked. Self-preservation took over, and he turned inward. Tom felt like he was caught up in a whirlwind. His instincts kicked in, and he quickly moved to automatic mode—no matter what, he wouldn't say anything that might get him into more trouble. While the company claimed that learning from mistakes was important, he didn't feel that was Lynn's intent. He felt cornered—attacked—and it was time to hunker down and survive. When the local boss called Tom into his office and pointedly asked if he had indeed fully fulfilled his obligations, Tom answered with great confidence: "Absolutely!" Internally, he had begun to doubt himself, but now wasn't the moment to share that. The need of the moment was to defend himself, protect his reputation, and project confidence. Tom left the office, went back to his own space, and continued spinning.

Jill

In the weeks post-vacation, Jill found herself struggling with Byron. When he joined the team as an experienced addition, everyone expected he could hit the ground running. Over the past few weeks, however, Jill saw signs that he was struggling. He avoided trainings, refused to read policies ("I know what I'm doing"), and failed to click with the rest of the team. As in most organizations, Byron was in a probationary period, and she started preparing for an outcome she hoped to avoid: Byron's termination.

Jill's stress rose as she tried without success to fix the situation. When her boss noticed her increased tension, she said it wasn't a big deal—she just had a lot on her mind. Jill was known for fixing things quickly, and the company's slow walk of anything HR-related made her even more anxious.

THINK AND DISCUSS (PART TWO)

1. What pressures exist in your world? Which are chronic? Acute?
2. Consider your family and coworkers—what pressures do they face?
3. When others experience stress, what behaviors do you observe?
4. When you face pressures, how do you act?

Ethan

Ethan's 5k best was around 23 minutes as he entered his senior year of cross country, and he set a personal goal of breaking 20 minutes. His coach supported him, saying that proper training would get Ethan there. Halfway through the season, things didn't look hopeful. Ethan's legs constantly hurt, perhaps the result of an undiagnosed injury. Off the trail, he was applying to colleges, navigating a heavy course load, and the required scholarship essays all pushed him beyond his comfort zone. He still believed in his goal of breaking 20 minutes and didn't want to fall short. With each successive meet, his flywheel spun faster earlier in the day to the point that he struggled to focus on anything else.

Ethan found a way to manage his physical pain, and that seemed to help his funk. He still felt discomfort during and after training, but the pain wasn't any worse during his actual run. While that encouraged him, his goal still felt beyond reach. He tried to maintain his positivity for everyone around him, but his worries kept building each day. He became so consumed by anxiety on race days that he could barely talk. And the feeling of crashing after waves of emotion building up to races tore him apart. Physically, emotionally, and mentally, he was drained. Meet days became his worst days.

Tom

Tom reached out to friends and colleagues to make sense of events. Although he received all kinds of advice, he had a hard time stopping his head from spinning enough to sleep. He was a wreck. How could a great career spanning almost two decades suddenly be challenged? How could an accusation get so serious so fast? Did no one believe him? After Lynn's visit, he heard nothing for two weeks, which felt like the longest two weeks of his life. He started journaling to calm his head. He touched base every day with close friends, seeking support and a safe place to process. Tom's thoughts ranged from quitting to fighting back to ignoring the situation, impulses he sometimes felt all at the same time. His team sensed he was off. His wife watched him fret and worry. No one knew how to help.

Then the conversations suddenly started up again. His boss, Lynn, Lynn's boss, and other leaders were suddenly questioning Tom nonstop. Some conversations felt like interrogations. Tom found himself repeating what he knew over and over to the point he wondered if he should get a lawyer. People told him to be honest—that honesty was the way to go—but he wasn't sure. He knew of other people who had disappeared from the company quickly for no apparent reason. He wondered if people wanted him gone. But why? He's been great for two decades! Why did it feel like people were out to get him?

Maybe Tom wasn't as good a leader as he thought. Or as good as everyone had told him all these years. He began questioning the deepest parts of himself—his worth, his beliefs, and his ingrained practices. This turmoil went on for months. Someone reached out to Tom with questions almost every day, often the same inquiries over and over. It felt like the organization was playing a game with him, waiting for him to give up and go away.

Jill

Jill found herself in the HR office with Byron, having taken all the steps to document that Byron wasn't performing well. He needed to step up or step out. The conversation was brief. Jill made her points, the HR person asked a few clarifying questions, and Byron simply sat unresponsive. When the meeting was all but finished, Byron launched into his own accusations against Jill. Accusations that pointed to Jill's sharing of her vacation experiences.

Jill was dumbfounded. What was Byron talking about? There was nothing that could substantiate Byron's claims. The meeting ended quickly, and Byron stayed and spoke with the HR person. Jill started what became a journey of random meetings and conversations with all kinds of people in the organization. She tried to seek resolution, find finality, and close the loop on Byron's claims, yet was repeatedly told the situation was under review. She struggled to grasp how a company that proclaimed itself employee-focused and people-centered could allow this "investigation" to go on for many months. Each day that went by without closure only increased Jill's anxiety.

THINK AND DISCUSS (PART THREE)

1. How can we take care of ourselves when we feel stressed?
2. What can we do to recognize when others are anxious?
3. How can we care for others experiencing worries?
4. How can we make anxiety a part of our daily conversations?

***Just as anxiety is highly personal, our responses
and outcomes vary immensely.***

Tom

How did it turn out for Tom? Eventually, the company went silent and acted like nothing ever happened. All the conversations with all the people just stopped. Tom's boss met his questions about the interrogations with re-direction and silence. Lynn showed up periodically and pretended like time had rolled back and things were back to the same old, same old. Tom still feels stung by how the organization handled the situation. He contemplates how people can behave contrary to their values and culture—and simply move on. While he's no longer in shock or complete self-protective mode, he brings heightened awareness to work each day. He's more protective, defensive, and less trusting of those around him.

Jill

After hanging on for more than six months without clarity, Jill finally quit. Her feelings of frustration and uncertainty were too much. If the company wanted her out—fine, she would go. Jill went around in her head and with her spouse about everything going on, and together they concluded that if the organization couldn't be forthright about their intentions, then they didn't want to be part of the place. Because Jill's spouse also worked for the same company, they both decided to exit. While they couldn't control the organization, they could choose to leave a culture that wasn't as employee-centric as they were led to believe. They made the difficult decision to leave to stay true to their values, including a priority of protecting their mental health.

Ethan

Ethan's teammates certainly noticed a change in Ethan from a high-flying, happy runner to an athlete overtaken by his inner self on meet days. Someone suggested he try music—putting in earbuds as soon as school let out and running through playlists, an approach Ethan tried the very next meet. As soon as the last bell rang, he plugged in. He kept his music flowing during stretches and warmups. He only removed his earbuds at the last possible moment, exactly eight minutes prior to the race start. After the race, he reflected on the tactic. While the flywheel started to spin up when he shut off his music, it didn't have time to reach critical speed, and the spinning slowed to a near stop once the race began. Ethan made music a permanent part of race day and went on to achieve his goal of a sub-20-minute 5k.

These stories reinforce the truth that anxiety exists in our worlds, and while we might slow its development, it's very difficult to shut it out altogether. However, we can recognize these facts: Some things are in our control, some are not, and no one has it all figured out.

When we share with others what makes us or is making us anxious... learn that others also experience anxiety...and commit to working through our anxious moments together...we begin to find just a hint of peace that can slow our own flywheels of anxiety.

CHAPTER 6

Recognition

CONSIDER THIS TYPICAL SCENARIO FROM THE WORLD OF CONSTRUCTION, WHERE DESIGNERS, PROJECT MANAGERS, SUPERINTENDENTS, TRADES, AND SUPPLIERS PUT IN MASSIVE HOURS TO DELIVER A HOSPITAL PROJECT.

The new operating room space was complex, wedging an operating room, processing areas, patient waiting rooms, offices, and conference rooms into one of the hospital's oldest areas, the most unlikely choice imaginable. The project team labored on the design for months, working tirelessly on a project that presented all kinds of challenges.

Sam, a new operating room director, saw the project as a chance to prove herself. She made herself the center of attention, insisting on attending every meeting and making every decision on behalf of the hospital staff. As the project neared completion, she asked for additional changes. "Now isn't the time," the team informed her. "We're a few weeks from opening, and modifications won't be easy or inexpensive," Sam complained to her supervisors, who demanded that her wishes be followed without impacting the opening date or cost. As always, the team came together and found paths to incorporate the changes, which required enormous teamwork, coordination, and collaboration.

Just weeks later, the room opened with great celebration. Festivities started with a ribbon-cutting, followed by tours and lunches. Sam posted online nonstop about the launch, featuring herself, physicians, and hospital leadership. The vibe was all about "We came together, we worked hard, and we got it done. We overcame! We conquered! Yay us!"

Notably absent from the celebrations and recognitions was the project delivery team that did the work. The designers. The engineers. The people who physically worked in the hospital hanging drywall, pulling cable, installing medical equipment. For nearly nine months, the team sacrificed time off—even weekends—and put in crazy overtime to deliver the new space. When I asked the designers, contractors, and project manager if it bothered them to be excluded, their response was unanimous. "I've built rooms, additions, and entire buildings for years," or as some pointed out, for decades. "I never get included in the opening ceremonies or celebrations."

The takeaway for the team leadership was clear. No more "Whatever it takes." Never again would they do delivery like this. The project weighed heavily on the people getting it done, with family activities missed, personal health sacrificed, and mental and physical well-being overlooked. The project leaders said, "We can do better. We owe it to ourselves and those we lead to be better."

Fast forward a few years. Many projects had been delivered by the same key people without repeating or requiring a big push at the end. It was good people, focus, connections, processes—projects going as planned. No overtime, scrambling, hectic weeks, or missed family activities. A consistent focus on health and well-being. Each project has a small celebration, such as a team lunch, happy hour, or the final meeting, where folks get to kick back and enjoy the fruits of their efforts. And guess what else? No grandiose celebrations and no high fives from outside the project team.

It's alarming that we celebrate the big push, where people lose precious things like time with their families to get the job done, yet we fail to celebrate when people consistently deliver.

What's the thought process? That we don't recognize people for doing their jobs? That a paycheck is recognition enough? From time to time, we say thank you for tasks completed, and we're sure to end every email with a hearty "Thanks!" or "I appreciate you." But does that meet our human need for recognition? Just a mumbled thanks for "showing up"?

THINK AND DISCUSS (PART ONE)

Think of three occasions when you have been recognized:
- What did you do?
- How was the recognition provided?
- How did it make you feel?
- Did the recognition influence your actions afterwards in any way?

Research shows that recognition directly impacts engagement and retention, two crucial factors for success and sustainability in today's workplace.

Gallup notes that only 3 in 10 employees strongly agree that they have received praise or recognition for a job well done within the past seven days. Achievers—a software firm that provides organizations with a tool to collect and manage recognition—states "employees that receive monthly vs. quarterly recognition are 36% more likely to say they are productive and engaged, and 22% more likely to be committed to their jobs." Harvard Business Review finds that the key to keeping employees engaged, productive, and loyal to an organization is recognition. HBR states that managers who excel at giving positive recognition are substantially more engaged than those who weren't recognized in the same way. Additionally, employees who receive strong recognition from leaders tend to have higher confidence, function as top performers, and are less likely to leave their jobs. Conversely, McKinsey has found that employees who feel undervalued are disengaged and often leave their jobs. Moreover, the recognition through one-time bonuses is perceived as transactional and impersonal and fails to resonate on a deep level.

Human Resources, industry associations, and research firms all highlight recognition as valuable, if not necessary. What is lacking, however, are examples of meaningful recognition. What is worthy of recognition? And what should recognition look like?

Consider your current setting. What recognition have you received lately—or maybe not so lately? Why did you receive the recognition?

Sometimes recognition is for doing things outside the norms of a job, like "Thanks for staying late and getting that thing done." "Appreciate you coming in this weekend." "Thanks for jumping in and helping that person—I know that's not part of your regular job." "It was awesome you volunteered."

At other times, recognition highlights everyday tasks, as in "Thanks for doing your job the other day. It helps the rest of us do our jobs." "Thanks for fixing the air conditioning." "You did a great job running the meeting." "Nice work on that presentation."

How do those comments land? Does it matter whether our extra effort gets noticed? Is it important to say thanks for fulfilling basic duties?

Increasing the volume of recognition doesn't make it more meaningful. Although many leaders believe that quantity is one path to success, just blasting "thanks for this" and "thanks for that" clearly isn't the answer. Various organizations adopted formal recognition tracking systems and report out who sent the most recognition in the past week and month. What's often missing are answers to basic questions: What should we be recognizing people for, and how should we show them recognition?

We know how we like to be recognized and often project that same expectation onto others. If we like the spotlight, we assume others do too. If we prefer quiet, personal recognition without any fanfare, again, we assume others appreciate the same. Yet what we like to be recognized for can vary from person to person just as much as how we are recognized. Failing to thoughtfully consider what is recognized and how recognition happens can cause it to backfire and badly miss. Examples:

- **One-time events:** Praising the last-minute score, the months of sacrifice to achieve a target, or going above and beyond a person's role sets the bar for everyone else. It screams, "If you want to get noticed, do your job well AND do a lot more."
- **Favoritism:** The organization repeatedly recognizes the same people over and over.
- **Lack of transparency:** When it isn't clear why recognition is being given, employees are unsure how to earn recognition.
- **Embarrassment:** When you recognize someone in public who prefers private acknowledgment, the recipient feels awkward and might question your intent.
- **Targets, metrics, and goals:** If your company embraces a quantity approach to recognition, then employees catch on quickly and wonder if the recognition is just an attempt to check a box.
- **Token gestures and gifts:** Small, meaningless rewards (tote bags, Bluetooth speakers, key chains, and other useless swag) make no

meaningful personal impact.

- **Delayed recognition:** Random praise for something done six months ago comes across as a complete afterthought.
- **Overdoing recognition:** Excessively praising an accomplishment, act, or task leads people to ignore the recognition and instead see the praise as fake and inauthentic.

In my first book, *Powerful Conversations*, I touched on Recognition in the chapter on Gratitude:

Recognition of a team member for "going above and beyond" is a dangerous form of recognition. The message it sends to others is that here, where we work, the way to get the attention of the boss is to do more than your job. This is like recognizing the big play—the last-second shot that wins the game, or the long touchdown throw. These one-off events, when recognized, are then noted by employees as the only thing to do to get attention. Recognition needs to extend to the consistent play, the blocking and tackling, the defending for 47 minutes before the last-second shot, the daily tasks and activities that keep everything moving forward. Without these, the one-offs simply don't happen.

How do you provide solid, meaningful, and impactful recognition?

Dig back into your childhood for an instance when your parents or siblings offered recognition. Dad said you did a nice job. Mom acknowledged how your hard work paid off. Your brother or sister made a comment that, despite its sarcasm, came from the heart.

Now, picture that happening in your adult world of work. You might hear or say the same words, but they don't make the same impact. Why? For recognition to feel meaningful—more than a transaction—the receiver must believe the person giving the recognition genuinely cares about them as a person.

Take Caryn, a processing clerk who feels her job doesn't involve much that would be considered exciting or deserving of recognition. She processes contracts and invoices. She stares at a computer all day, occasionally talking on the phone, though handling most of her tasks via email. Sure, she steps up to coordinate work parties, get-togethers, and holiday celebrations. And she gets recognition for it. She doesn't do those "above and beyond" things for the recognition but because she likes to. Seeing others happy is what drives her.

Caryn doesn't like attention for these extras, and it drives her crazy when her efforts are publicly recognized. Her boss instead recognizes her for her outstanding work in the core duties of her job—her consistency, her reliability, and her importance to the team—and he offers this affirmation in smaller settings. Without Caryn executing contracts, work would stop. Without her processing invoices, people wouldn't get paid, and families would go without basic needs. His words connect with the meaning of her work, and he offers this very personalized recognition regularly. Caryn feels her boss understands what's important to her, and even if his words aren't perfect, they hit home with deep feeling.

THINK AND DISCUSS (PART TWO)

- What kind of recognition feels most meaningful to you—for the work you do, for your efforts at home, for who you are?
- How can you make recognition a regular part of your life
  - At work?
  - At home?
  - In your community?
- Where can you expand the circle of people you recognize?
- Recognize someone right now. Reach out and let them know a specific reason you are recognizing them.

While recognition makes us feel good, history and philosophy teach us that actively seeking recognition from others isn't something to strive for.

Many schools of thought say that while we should strive to be worthy of appreciation and recognition, we shouldn't be concerned with whether we receive them. Doing the right thing because it's the right thing is important. The recognition that might or might not follow is not.

How do we recognize others in meaningful ways? Start with these steps:

1. **Build a relationship.** Only when you focus on understanding what matters to that person can you begin to comprehend what to recognize.
2. **Recognize consistency.** These are often things that must be performed consistently—and maybe feel boring! Kids build good habits like brushing teeth, doing homework, and sleeping well with constant

reinforcement through recognition. The same is true at work. Reliability, consistency, and daily activities done well need recognition.

3. **Understand what kinds of recognition people appreciate.** Not everyone likes a handwritten card. For me to write a card would be out of character. I instead make time for coffee or a one-on-one conversations. Others appreciate me showing up at a team or group meeting to provide public recognition that comes from my heart and demonstrates I know them deeply.

4. **Focus on quality, not quantity.** How much recognition you provide is nowhere near as important as the quality of what you say and do.

THINK AND DISCUSS (PART THREE)

- Who can you recognize today for who they are?
- Where can you learn more about the people around you and what type of recognition they desire?
- Where can you influence others to recognize who people are instead of the actions and results they achieve?
- How can you move others toward providing more meaningful and personal recognition?

People like recognition—being acknowledged for who they are and things they do. Craving and obsessing over recognition is a difficult and dangerous situation.

No one denies that it feels good to be recognized. Yet people who experience the high of attention and basking in the spotlight can struggle when the good feelings fade.

Recognition triggers dopamine in our brains. This neurotransmitter, connected to reward and pleasure, reacts to recognition as a positive reinforcement for our actions, and we feel valued and appreciated. Social media platforms are experts in manipulating our dopamine triggers through views, likes, comments, and shares. We experience reinforcement of our actions, and positive responses make us feel great.

It's the same at work and at home. Research on dopamine also says these reactions are more impactful and meaningful when we receive them from someone we care about—meaning recognition from an employee, teammate, leader, family member, or friend perceived to care about you as a person will have a much greater impact. It doesn't matter in what way, shape, or form the recognition arrives.

When you celebrate your kid's victory in a sport, however meaningless the game, your recognition goes straight to their heart. Why? Because they know you care about them. When you acknowledge your spouse for cooking dinner, cleaning the house, or having a great day at work, the same recognition from anyone else feels less impactful because that person doesn't care about them like you do.

Recognition triggers a chemical reaction inside us. But recognition from those who know us best ignites a feeling, an emotion, and a connection that transcends the physical and creates even stronger bonds between us. That's the recognition we love to receive, and the skillfully delivered recognition we need to provide.

CHAPTER 7

Compassion

**DON'T BRING YOUR STUFF TO WORK.
DON'T BE TOO TALKATIVE, TOO PERSONAL,
OR TOO INVOLVED. THERE'S WORK TO DO.
WE DON'T HAVE TIME TO TRULY CARE.**

Even if we haven't heard those exact words, we've probably felt the need to "keep it professional" at work. If you want an ear, talk to your spouse or a friend. On your own time.

When COVID ravaged the world, many managers were suddenly thrust into the unknown. Their usual routines consisted of goal setting, reports, and process conversations mixed with a smattering of small talk and occasional one-on-ones. Yet managers suddenly were talking with team members about personal health, sick family, anxiety, fear, workplace safety, and the politics of the epidemic. Managers became more than managers. They were forced into the role of friend, fellow humans traversing a strange new world with their direct reports.

Managers also found themselves deliberating with their peers on how to navigate topics previously off limits. Some managers embraced the human-centric focus as an important dynamic often missing in the workplace. Others felt overwhelmed with stress and anxiety.

Shawn found himself sitting with a tearful team member, each wearing a mask. *This wasn't in my job description,* he thought. The team member went on and on about sick parents, a hospitalized cousin battling COVID, and neighbors who didn't believe the virus was real. When the team member confessed that the constant distractions kept him from getting his work done, Shawn wondered how he was supposed to respond. A few months prior, he would have considered the array of motivational tools he could use to push his team to perform. Now, performance measures suddenly weren't as important. Or at least that's what he was hearing from above him in the organization. But how could he set aside performance? Work needs to get done, no matter what's going on in the world.

Later that day, Shawn went home and found that his wife felt ill. *Maybe it's this COVID thing.* By morning, his wife was barely able to breathe and was complaining of chest pains. He called the doctor's office and was told he should take his wife to the emergency room if other symptoms arise. In the meantime, she should quarantine for 14 days. Shawn couldn't take 14 days off to care for her, but she certainly wasn't well enough to care for herself. He had to devise a way to work and be there for his wife.

Shawn's first call that morning was yet another virtual chat. Like yesterday, he found himself face-to-face with a team member whose close friend had fallen ill. With his own wife sick, Shawn suddenly felt like his role as manager no longer mattered. He was just one human talking with another, listening to what was going on in what used to be a highly personal and compartmentalized world.

This story played out millions of times around the world. During COVID, virtual meetings made room for human elements—dogs barking, kids in the background, lax dress codes, and, in some cases, a bit of fun. Jobs were still serious, yet our ability to bring elements of our lives into each other's worlds just sort of happened. And it felt good.

And then COVID ended. More accurately, case counts temporarily fell, and impatience with restrictions rose. I was on a leadership video call when a participant's dog barked. The person speaking stopped and said, "Would you all please mute yourselves? The background noise is distracting." This wasn't an important meeting or a speaker addressing a large audience. But it was the moment we officially killed the human-centric environment we created during the pandemic. We were back to the old normal. We had things to get done. So don't bring your personal business to work.

It felt like the end of a brief stint of compassion.

THINK AND DISCUSS (PART ONE)

- How do you define compassion?
- What does compassion look like?
- What does compassion feel like when you give it—and receive it?
- Do people show compassion at work? With whom? When? Why?

> **Compassion is defined as recognizing that another person is suffering and a desire to relieve that pain.**

Is compassion when a kid gets a cut, and a parent cleans the cut and puts a bandage on? Or when someone is suffering the emotional pain of a break-up, and another tries to make the person feel better? Or when a colleague is hurt by being overlooked for a promotion, and you step in to help them process their disappointment?

Yes, yes, and yes.

The gist of compassion seems obvious, yet it's easily confused with other emotions and motivations. It's neither sympathy nor empathy. Sympathy is feeling sorry for a person, and empathy is entering into the person's pain. Compassion not only recognizes that someone is hurting but also actively seeks to ease suffering. And when we receive true compassion, we know it. It feels significant when others act to help us.

Naturally, we're compassionate toward those we care about. When a loved one suffers, we want to help. Most people also naturally react with compassion to a sudden, obvious need. When a stranger trips and falls, others step in to help that person back up.

How about our ability to express compassion at work? Why can that feel difficult or even impossible?

Early in his career, Shawn was extremely compassionate. In his first job during high school, his coworkers regarded him as a great listener. One person would go on and on about his problems, and Shawn would listen intently. He had never experienced anything like what was being shared by his coworker. He was fascinated. Until his own work suffered. This person's issues became a distraction, leading to Shawn getting a stern lecture from his boss. Shawn finally had to tell his coworker to back off.

Shawn had begun to develop a shield of cool behaviors he activated whenever someone did what he considered to be oversharing. If anyone took up time that impacted his work output, he raised his shield. It rarely took long before the speaker received the message. Shawn wasn't any less compassionate, but it was now heavily guarded.

Once, in his late twenties, Shawn came to work to discover a coworker visibly shaken. The person's dog had died unexpectedly the evening before, and the coworker was barely keeping it together, with moments of calm shattered by sobbing. Shawn's entire workgroup felt so bad that they took turns comforting the employee. By noon, the employee was doing better, and everyone was back at work. Shawn found the team's compassion admirable, yet he wondered why it took losing a pet to demonstrate care to be okay at work.

What does it mean to be human on the job? Many companies claim you can be yourself at work. They sell their culture as fun-filled days of team building, friendship, and happy hours. Is this real? If it is, is it enough?

Let's push deeper. What does it mean for work culture to be truly human-centric? Are you able to:

- Be sad from time to time, even for no apparent reason?
- Not have your life perfectly together?
- Admit you're unsure or confused?
- Feel ugly some days and cute other days?
- Be unprepared for how things turn out?
- Have tough days?
- Show unhappiness?
- Fluctuate in weight?
- Be productive some days and less on others?

What happens when you or others display any of these realities? Are you still embraced? Do others seek to understand how you feel? Can team members spend time being compassionate with each other without fearing how it might temporarily impact work?

Does the severity of someone's issue dictate how much compassion you can bring? How about if someone's loved one dies, or a pet dies, or a teenager breaks up with their partner? What warrants time and attention?

THINK AND DISCUSS (PART TWO)

- How do you practice compassion at work?
- What do we mean when we say, "Everybody makes mistakes" or "We learn from failure"? Are failures a learning process at your workplace?
- What's the difference between compassion and self-compassion?
- Do you have self-compassion? How do you know? What does it look and feel like?

Some people seem naturally in tune when others need their compassion. Some can even easily spot when others suffer from poor self-compassion.

Megan finished delivering a presentation and was debriefing with a friend. Megan said she felt the presentation went well enough, but she could have done so much better in multiple areas—content, delivery, presence, and so on. Megan wasn't happy with her body language and how she stood during the presentation. She reflected on how much better her slides could have looked. Her friend stopped her mid-sentence and said, "Don't talk about my friend Megan like that!" The friend recognized that Megan wasn't engaging in healthy reflection but was instead beating herself up with negative self-talk.

Her friend spotted Megan's suffering and stepped in to confront and relieve it. Though Megan's suffering wasn't external—like losing a pet—her internal struggles were painful. She was missing an opportunity to practice self-compassion.

Consider three components of self-compassion:

1. **Mindfulness:** Recognizing you're stressed or struggling without judging yourself or over-reacting.
2. **Self-Kindness:** Putting aside harsh self-criticism to show support and understanding toward yourself.
3. **Connectedness:** Remembering you're not alone in making mistakes and experiencing difficulties. We've all been there.

There's a line between self-critique for your own improvement and beating yourself up. Statements like "I'm so stupid!" and "What's wrong with me?" are signals of a struggle to exercise self-compassion. The suffering isn't always obvious. Self-deprecation often happens internally, which requires extra attention to notice.

CliftonStrengths offers insight into people's varying abilities to see and respond to suffering. Those with strengths in Empathy, Connectedness, and Relator are more likely to naturally recognize when others are suffering. They read the signs, feel what people are putting out, and are more likely to discern when someone needs compassion. Others, like those who have Responsibility and Achiever, for example, are less likely to see the signs unless a person deliberately communicates the cause of their pain. Even then, people with these strengths may prioritize work or action over other people's feelings.

This makes it sound like people who have certain strengths are jerks. That's absolutely not the case. When we're wired in a way that puts action, achievement, and to-do lists first, we will often overlook feelings and emotions. Is that bad? No. If you're slow to recognize when others are suffering and need compassion, then you can do a couple of things. One is to let people know how you naturally see the world. Another is to seek ways to remind yourself to ask if action is what's needed at this moment.

THINK AND DISCUSS (PART THREE)

- What type of language do you use internally when you make a mistake or disappoint yourself?
- How do you help someone who might be overcome with negative self-talk? How can you uncover the kind of help they might need?
- How do you recognize someone needs encouragement to show self-compassion?
- How can you partner with others to create an environment that supports practicing compassion? How can you recognize and reward people for being compassionate?

Being a friend, a colleague, or a coworker who cares is as much about who you are and how you act as an individual as it is the environment and culture of your workplace.

A doctor arrived at the hospital early in the morning, happy he beat traffic. He hit the ground running, excited about the day ahead. Typical day, for sure, though today would be more intense than others. After a few minutes checking email, he gathered his team and discussed morning to-dos. He was assigned to the emergency department today, and as he crossed the lobby, an elderly woman reached out and touched his arm. The doctor turned and asked if he could help. She inquired if he was Dr. Antonio.

"Yes, that's me," he said. "What can I do for you?"

The woman was there with her husband, who was admitted a few minutes ago. The doctor said he hoped all was well with him.

"That's not why I stopped you," she said. "I recognize you from a few years ago. You worked on my son. He was admitted with a gunshot wound, and you saved his life."

The doctor was stunned, slightly embarrassed, and not quite sure what to say. All he could mutter was "I'm glad I could help."

"He's dead now," she replied. "Another gunshot. Nothing anybody could do about it. But thank you for saving him the first time."

"I'm sorry to hear that," the doctor said. "Take care." He hurried back to his office, where he sat down and sighed with relief at escaping the woman. But he felt a mess of emotions. Was he wrong to leave so quickly? Did she want more from him? Probably—but he left. Should he go back? What would he say? Did she need counseling? He has work to do. He doesn't have time. That's why the hospital has counselors. But why was he so worked up? He knew that running away was wrong. He could have sat the woman down and talked. He could have said so much more. Darn it. That woman needed him, and he let her down. His own embarrassment got in the way of helping. He felt challenged, uncomfortable, and he ran away. He failed.

The doctor was startled by a knock on his door. A colleague leaned in and said he had been trying to get the doctor's attention for the past five minutes. Was everything alright?

"Yes, of course," the doctor said.

The colleague didn't buy it. "Well, obviously not," he said. The colleague took a seat, looked the doctor in the eye, and told him to start at the beginning.

No matter where we work and no matter the norms around compassion, we can choose to create moments where feelings don't need to be left at the door. We can allow time for compassion, seek opportunities to show it, and demonstrate how compassion and self-compassion can be part of our everyday lives.

CHAPTER 8

Grief

TO ME, THE BED WAS JUST A BED. TO MY SON, IT WAS THE ONLY PART OF THE WORLD THAT WAS TOTALLY HIS. IN AN INSTANT, I RIPPED THAT AWAY.

My son was three when he graduated to a big boy bed. We bought him a cool frame with a canopy that looked like the starry sky. At first, the bed was situated the usual way, with the mattress about a foot above the floor. When my son turned five, we flipped the bed and it became a loft three feet off the ground, high enough underneath for a small desk, a few toys, and a string of lights dangling from the frame. A light blanket hung like a tent flap made the space his own little hideout. I squeezed in there with him a couple of times to hang out while he played a game or worked on a project, but it was truly his space. That bed was the first possession that was truly his, something no one else in our family could share.

Just after my son turned six, we moved to a new house. He was too tall for the bed, so I listed it for sale. Another family would pick it up one evening, and I told him we needed to disassemble it. When he asked why, I told him he was getting a bigger bed for the new house. He was devastated. His bed—his hideout, his own space—was going away. It didn't matter that the new bed was a better fit—bigger and higher, with dresser drawers for his stuff. He felt the emotional pain of his world changing dramatically, suddenly, without warning, and the situation was beyond his control. It was his first experience with deep, meaningful grief.

At age 33, I had a newborn, no savings, a house that was way too expensive, and a job I knew was coming to an end. While the residential development company had survived the initial real estate crash six months earlier, there was no way the company could keep me on the payroll forever. With a bit of foresight, I spent half of each day working and the other half job hunting. I landed a handful of interviews, traveled across the country to speak with different companies, and endured six months of repeated rejections. Always the same story. "We decided to hold off on filling this position at this time," they all said. "Thanks and good luck to you. We'll let you know if anything changes."

Three months later, I lost my job. The company closed, and I was jobless. I saw it coming for as much as a year, and I believed I could quickly find another job. Just a few weeks on unemployment, doubling down on my search, and I would be working again. My loss of employment motivated me even more to get out there and find something better. I felt sad for just a moment. I told myself to buckle up, bury my unhappiness, and get to work. I didn't have time to feel sorry for myself.

THINK AND DISCUSS (PART ONE)

- How do people respond to grief?
- How do people respond to loss?
- What kinds of grief have you personally experienced—around possessions, people, relocating, status, influence, power, sudden versus foreseen? How did you respond?
- How has the impact of grief and your reactions to it changed over time?

I'm not wired to allow myself to experience grief. It's part nature, part nurture, and a major gap I needed to learn to deal with.

All my jobs after college were in residential construction, building houses, apartment complexes, and light commercial properties. In 2007, the industry shut down nationwide for a solid two years. Thousands of people just like me were out of work. At first, I spent entire days job hunting. I beat the street, searched online, and called everyone I knew. Then I would exercise to relieve stress, then help with the family. Days turned into weeks that stretched into months. I stopped paying the mortgage because we were out of money, and when the foreclosure notice was taped to our front door, I was livid. Crazy, over-the-top angry that I almost exploded. Then I broke down and cried. All the grief that had built up inside me for the past year needed to be released, to burst from the deepest cavern in my gut where I had buried it, that dark place where I had been taught to shove my feelings. Feelings don't matter. Leave them at the door. Feeling bad? Call your mom. We got work to do. Get it done. Don't be weak.

I was in a stupor. I couldn't bear to look at my laptop or talk to anyone. The grief of losing my house, my things, my job, and my sense of self was so powerful that it halted me in my tracks. I did nothing for two full days. I had never experienced feelings that overwhelmed me and took over my entire heart, mind, and body. Then I slowly started to do things again. My thoughts felt less out of control, and here and there, my attitude and drive would pop back up.

What I discovered firsthand was that grief doesn't simply go away. It needs to be worked through, processed, and fixed, not buried or ignored. But I still felt that any form of sitting and being sad was unproductive and weak. I wanted to pick up a book or read a step-by-step guide to get me through this as fast as possible. Acknowledge, process, do the steps, and move forward. Take a year to grieve a loss? That was a foreign concept.

When I was a kid, we had a big family in Chicago. Lots of relatives and lots of funerals, all the same. A hushed viewing at the funeral home, followed the next day by a tearful church service, a drive to the gravesite, and a reception where everyone loosened up and smiles returned. I once asked my mom if she was sad that a relative had passed, and she said death is a part of life. It happens. You move on. Very matter-of-fact.

As humans, if we don't process grief, we typically engage in one of three unhealthy responses: avoidance, suppression, and guilt.

- **Avoidance:** Instead of embracing the grief within us, we bury it. We don't talk about it, acknowledge it, or allow it to impact our thoughts and actions. We think that avoiding and ignoring our loss will make it go away.

- **Suppression:** We sense the dark feelings inside us, yet we do our best to cover them up with other feelings. We act happy to keep our grief and sadness out of sight and mind.
- **Guilt:** Grief happens, and when it does, we tell ourselves the event that evoked grief is our fault. We made the bad thing happen, or at least didn't prevent it. We brought it on ourselves. We deserve to feel bad, so we beat ourselves up.

Whether we're an introvert or an extrovert, we discover that society doesn't encourage external processing of grief. When a coworker says they feel sad because their mom suddenly fell ill and might die, most people don't really know what to say or do. Unless we have a naturally high sense of compassion or empathy, we run out of ideas beyond attempting to utter a few nice words or perhaps send a note. We feel bad for the person and their situation. We may awkwardly try to share our own relatable experience. The reality is that no HR process, training, or educational opportunity teaches us how to respond in a human-centric way that encourages externally processing grief.

In workplaces and family culture and dynamics, there may be a strong view that productivity is important, and if you need a bereavement day, take it. But don't bring your emotions to a staff meeting. Your personal business is your business, not ours. Deal with it. Sure, we feel for you. But come back once you get over it. Better yet, deal with it on your own time. This sounds harsh, and hopefully, your family and place of work aren't this way. What surprises me is how often companies say they place their people first, yet their actions don't support the people-first approach.

Those long hours at work that we practice putting a lid on our grief trains us to withhold feelings and attempt to process them internally if at all. Maybe it feels okay to talk about a death, but not for more than a day or two. And openly discussing the varieties of grief inflicted by work is often off limits. Passed over for a promotion? No one wants to listen to you complain. Sudden transfer to a different office or city? Be happy you have a job. Didn't win a contract? Hunker down, figure out why your team didn't win, improve the process, and apply the lessons to the next one. Want to feel bad about losing? Suck it up! We don't have time to feel bad. There's the next job to win. Don't waste time crying about losing.

Get the picture? Even at work—especially at work—we practice avoidance, suppression, and guilt. We convince ourselves that those are the correct ways to handle grief.

THINK AND DISCUSS (PART TWO)

- Is it possible to avoid grief altogether? Why—or why not?
- How were you raised to process grief?
- Do you process grief more internally or more externally? Does it differ whether the grief is sudden vs foreseen?
- Can people share grief safely? With whom? Where? When?

Grief can be sudden. It can sometimes be foreseen.
It definitely should be shared.

When you're renting a house and receive notice that the property is in foreclosure, you experience both sudden shock and an enduring hassle of finding another place to live and adjusting to new surroundings. When you see your company downsizing, and while you hope for the best, you get laid off. If you've ever been traumatized by a layoff, you know the grieving is a long road. Even if you find a new job quickly, you feel anguish for many months. You wonder why you were let go while others kept their jobs. What could you have done differently? Perform better? Deliver more? Work harder? Play more politics? The internal dialogues can go on and on, and often those around you don't even see your processing.

The curious thing about grief is this: Whatever you're going through, someone else is either going through it too or has gone through it. We rarely share about the times we grieved and how we changed through the process. And once we get through it, we say we're "back to normal." But we might be anything but normal. The experience changed us. When we emerge from our processing, we're not the same person.

When you have needed to process grief, have you found opportunities to safely share? I went through a year-long challenge that struck out of nowhere and caused major life disruptions. I was lucky to have six people I could call, email, and text at any point to vent, seek advice, and talk through the happenings of the day—people willing to listen, ask questions, and, from time to time, give advice. The first step was me reaching out to two of them and saying I needed to talk. The second step was them encouraging me to talk to others and suggesting specific names. And they followed up with me, holding me accountable to grow my circle and share what I was going through.

In 1969, Elizabeth Kubler-Ross described one of the best-known grieving processes. Although her book On Death and Dying focused on people who experienced loss through death, the process applies to any type of loss. She outlined five linear stages:

- Denial: You have difficulty accepting that a loss is real.
- Anger: You feel anger and may direct it toward anyone or anything.
- Bargaining: You attempt to reach an agreement in your mind to avoid dealing with the loss.
- Depression: You may experience clinical depression.
- Acceptance: Eventually, most people embrace the loss, often while the pain is still there.

Reaching out for help is a struggle for many people. It might be a struggle for you. When people pass through denial, anger, bargaining, and depression, they rarely state openly and honestly that they're experiencing grief, grieving, or going through the process. Consider your answers to the first set of questions. When have you experienced grief? Did you openly share and seek support? Or did you focus internally, moving through the stages by yourself?

THINK AND DISCUSS (PART THREE)

- You should share and process your grief with others. How could you best do that?
- When we notice others experiencing grief and loss, how can we help them process their thoughts and emotions?
- What does supporting a grieving person look like in practical terms?
- Does our support change if the grief is sudden vs. foreseen?

When people grieve, they may need more help than you can provide. And when you are grieving, you might need professional support.

There's no right way to grieve. The process is highly individual. What isn't individual is letting people know you're in the process and being aware of when others are grieving. Harvard Medicine speaks of "prolonged grief," while the Mayo Clinic speaks of "complicated grief" when the grieving process persists or impairs daily life. There are rarely signs at first, though issues do develop. Changes in physical health, behavior, and relationships, as well as recurring and prolonged waves of sadness, all indicate someone may be stuck in the grieving process. When you see those signs in others or yourself, seek professional help.

At times, people experience grief that shuts them down for weeks, months, or even years. Knowing we aren't alone and having people to talk through what goes on inside us can make all the difference.

At our regular Saturday men's breakfast at church, I was facilitating a conversation on grief. We used the questions in this chapter as a guide, and after the second set of discussion questions, I asked, "How'd the conversation go?" One group said, "We're sharing more than we normally do, and as a table we're listening to each other. We usually don't talk about these things with people who aren't close to us, yet here we are. And it's good."

Indeed. It is good.

CHAPTER 9

Empathy

I DIDN'T ANTICIPATE DEEP LIFE INSIGHTS FROM AN ANIMATED CHILDREN'S MOVIE DEPICTING ANTHROPOMORPHIZED EMOTIONS MANAGING "HEADQUARTERS," THE CONTROL CENTER OF A GIRL'S MIND.

Pixar's *Inside Out* is more than a cute escape. As young Riley grows from child to teenager, the cartoon characters "Joy" and "Sadness" go on a journey within her, wandering through her past. Along the way, everyone learns profound new things.

Years earlier, Riley and her imaginary friend Bing Bong launched into adventures together aboard her little red wagon through space, to ocean depths, even back in time.

Joy and Sadness eventually meet Bing Bong in the chasm of Riley's mind, where faded memories and anything now considered useless get tossed—bits no longer needed to function, like the names of discarded Transformer toys or Atari games. As Riley nears the big jump to teendom, Bing Bong sees the red wagon headed to the scrap heap. Try as he might, he can't save the wagon, and he realizes his adventures with Riley are over. The defeated old friend cries out, "Riley can't be done with me!" Bing Bong is so distraught that he can't continue the adventure. Joy, true to her name, tries to cheer him up. She wants to fix him and move on. She tickles him, makes funny faces, and tries to make a game of the situation. Bing Bong just sits there.

Then, Sadness tells Bing Bong, "I'm sorry they took something you loved. It's gone." Joy exclaims, "Sadness, don't make it worse!" But Sadness continues listening to Bing Bong, acknowledging the weight of the event. Sadness looks as though she feels the same thing Bing Bong feels. She experiences the grief of losing the wagon just like Bing Bong does. She lets Bing Bong give her a hug and allows him to cry. After a few moments, he says, "I'm ok now," and they continue the adventure.

Joy is confused and asks Sadness what just happened. Sadness replies, "He was sad, so I listened." It was clear that Sadness invited that conversation by asking Bing Bong about the adventures he and Riley enjoyed, acknowledging the situation was painful, and giving him space to cry and be in the moment. Not only did she feel what he felt, but they faced sadness together.

That was empathy, pure and simple.

THINK AND DISCUSS (PART ONE)

- What is empathy?
- Where do you see empathy?
- Are you naturally empathetic?
- Where do you experience empathy?

Empathy is the ability to understand and share another person's feelings and experiences.

Empathy involves being able to see things from someone else's perspective and imagine what they might be thinking or feeling. The feeling we get when we are seen, felt, and understood is empathy in action.

Empathy is different from sympathy, which is feeling sorry for someone or pitying their situation. It's feeling moved by another person's feelings.

Empathy also differs from compassion, which comprehends what's happening, wants suffering to end, and takes the additional step of providing help. What the character Joy expressed was compassion. She saw someone who felt sad and acted to fix it.

With empathy, we understand and feel the other person's experience as if it were our own, but without experiencing it firsthand. Empathy doesn't involve doing something to alleviate the other person's suffering. It's more about sharing than fixing.

So where do we see empathy in our lives? And why is it so hard to put into practice?

I can offer a test case of how rare and difficult empathy really is. I helped host an online group session focused on empathy. My fellow leaders and I guided the group through three activities, ultimately leading participants to experience and extend empathy during the session.

We started with a simple challenge. Each person shared an example of seeing someone who needed empathy, yet they responded by 1) offering help that wasn't wanted, or 2) saying, "You could have had it so much worse. At least blah blah blah didn't happen!"

People got the point. Although it seems helpful—compassionate—to try to fix the suffering of others, it backfired. Likewise, when people one-up others, their effort to provide a broader context to a bad situation made the suffering person feel dismissed, ignored, or even resentful.

As the group went deeper, we explored the definition of empathy and its three common forms:

1. **Cognitive Empathy:** Putting yourself into someone else's shoes and seeing their perspective without engaging with their emotions.
2. **Emotional Empathy:** Feeling the other person's emotions alongside them, as if you had "caught" their emotions.
3. **Compassionate Empathy:** Feeling someone's pain and acting to help.

The timing of this group session was significant. It took place about six months into the COVID pandemic. In the days leading up to the event, many school districts made decisions about the upcoming school year, with some choosing to go back full-time, some part-time, and some remaining completely virtual.

As a parent with kids, I had spent six months being a teacher, parent, activity director, vacation planner, and summer camp organizer on top of my day job, and I secretly looked forward to my kids returning to school and regaining some sense of normal for everyone. At the same time, I was highly concerned about putting teachers, admins, and staff at risk. I certainly didn't want any harm to come to anyone.

When I learned that our district wasn't returning to in-person learning,

I experienced a rush of feelings: let down, disappointed, drained, and just spent. In the online session, I shared that participants had an opportunity to be empathetic towards parents who felt like I did.

As soon as the session ended, I got a note from a participant. "I don't have kids," it started, "so I can't imagine how much parents are dealing with right now. BUT..." It was the BUT that stood out. The person told me how hard it was to hear parents express feelings like mine while teachers were putting themselves at risk. The note was long, intense, and focused on how wrong I was—an ironic twist after our session of empathy.

Want to know a sure-fire way to NOT practice empathy? Tell someone their feelings are wrong.

Diligently echoing someone's feelings, followed by BUT invalidates how that person feels. Empathy involves entering into how another person feels, so labeling some feelings wrong isn't being empathetic.

Expressing empathy is so hard that a session focused on this quality isn't enough to erase old habits. It's too easy to return to normal life and leave empathy behind. Our brains zero in on our own priorities and point of view. Like Joy, we want to get on whatever comes next, and Bing Bong's sadness was in the way.

Empathy is especially difficult for two reasons.

Reason one: Empathy involves emotions. When someone feels angry or sad, being empathetic means you have to feel angry or sad. That's tough. Most of us want to avoid pain and unpleasant feelings such as anger and sadness, so by default, we don't want to go there.

Reason two: Empathy requires real effort. It's not easy to understand others and see the world through their eyes. In the movie, Sadness had enough information to know Bing Bong was sad about the end of his adventures with Riley. That fact was obvious. Our daily interactions with other humans, however, are rarely so clear. Understanding why someone is angry or sad may take effort, questions, and emotional sensitivity before relating to those emotions can really begin.

THINK AND DISCUSS (PART TWO)

- Why is empathy necessary?
- How can you be empathetic if you aren't naturally wired to perceive

what others feel?
- What does it mean to receive empathy?
- What does it feel like to be empathetic?

Empathy appears among the strengths denoted by CliftonStrengths. Of all 34 qualities, Empathy is one of the least common in the United States.

Here's how Gallup defines the Empathy Strength:

You can sense the emotions of those around you. You can feel what they are feeling as though their feelings are your own. Intuitively, you are able to see the world through their eyes and share their perspective. You do not necessarily agree with each person's perspective. You do not necessarily feel pity for each person's predicament—this would be sympathy, not empathy. You do not necessarily condone the choices each person makes, but you do understand. This instinctive ability to understand is powerful.

This definition offers insights into why empathy is hard. Which leads us to consider two more reasons.

Reason three: Being truly empathetic means we make space for the emotions, insights, and choices made by others. In other words, we must fight the urge to say things like "You shouldn't be angry at that," or "There's no reason to cry." Our internal judge is strong and wants to voice our opinions. While we can't stop judgments from forming inside us we can recognize when they are coming up and catch them before we speak!

Reason four: Empathy is challenging because of empathy overload. Issues like wars, political uncertainty, social injustice, and child starvation go on and on. It's impossible to be empathetic to all the issues in the world. Moreover, for people in professional roles requiring a high degree of empathy—fields like teaching, hospice, social work, and counseling—empathy is a way of life. Just as the person who works as a project manager might not want to plan what their family should do each weekend, people who spend their workdays being highly empathetic don't seek opportunities to be empathetic outside work.

Nevertheless, life presents many situations where we can exercise empathy.

When corporate initiatives negatively impact human beings, the opportunity to be empathetic is ripe. Take Stephan, who oversees a large facility.

One of his responsibilities was to ensure the fire alarm worked properly and was always up to code. He relied on a local contractor to inspect, maintain, upgrade, and repair their system.

The corporate folks one day decided that Stephan could no longer use that person. They planned to save money by centralizing this service for the entire organization. The local guy would be replaced by a larger firm from out of town.

The old provider was shocked by the sudden decision, and he eventually went out of business. That person certainly needed empathy. But so did Stephan. He found the new company difficult to work with. They were hard to contact. The workers who showed up weren't customer-focused and lacked the knowledge the previous person had gained over decades. And on multiple occasions, the alarm was incorrectly triggered in the middle of the night, and Stephan had to go to work and check it out.

When Stephan voiced concerns to his boss, he was told to "power through" and deal with "the normal side effects and challenges of large-scale change." Very corporate-like. Wasn't there an opportunity to be empathetic toward Stephan? He had a family, cared deeply about his site, and had to get up in the middle of the night on multiple occasions. He was mad, angry, frustrated, and irritated. Corporate folks told him it would get better.

What Stephan needed was an ear that acknowledged those feelings. He needed to know someone understood how he felt—without telling him he was wrong to feel that way or trying to fix him. The effort to save money looked good to the organization, but corporate folks told him to leave his feelings at the door. At one point, a corporate supervisor told Stephan, "I deal with facts, not feelings." And the perceived facts were that the change saved the organization money. But at what cost?

Do we need others to show us empathy at work? Do we need to extend empathy to others? Do we signal toughness with a no-tissue policy at work, as in "No crying here!" Or is there a way we can bring our whole selves to work—and let others do the same—and still excel at our jobs?

THINK AND DISCUSS (PART THREE)

- Where can you be more empathetic?
- What opportunities do you have right now to show empathy?

- How can you help others recognize opportunities to be more empathetic?
- How can you help others develop the skills to extend empathy?

Being aware of when someone needs you to be empathetic is the first step in improving your skills.

If you're not naturally empathetic, start by listening to verbal cues from others. Understand where their words come from.

You might hear and feel an experience like something you've faced, though don't try to force a connection between your experience and theirs. Seek to understand the situation by asking questions and considering how you would feel in the situation. Be present during the conversation—avoid all distractions. Change the environment if you need to. At work, get away from your phone and computer and find a place where you can focus solely on the other person. At home, find a quiet spot free from screens, other people, and pets. One of the most challenging aspects of empathy is listening so closely that you can express your understanding of what the other person has experienced. Only then can you truly share the other person's feelings.

Opportunities to practice empathy are random and certainly not rare. Perhaps you strike up a conversation with someone you know, yet haven't talked to in a while. That person overshares about how their kid is in trouble, making poor life choices during their first year of college, and the relationship between the kid and the parents is now very strained. Some people get scared off by someone's sudden openness and try to escape the conversation as fast as possible. That person is crying out for you to stick around and practice empathy. Lean in, listen, ask questions, and acknowledge feelings.

And here's a simple, instructive, memorable picture to keep in mind: There are times to be less like Joy and be more like Sadness!

CHAPTER 10

Culture

I CAUGHT THAT SOMETHING WAS UP JUST DAYS AFTER MY ARRIVAL AS A NEW HIRE AT A LARGE INSTITUTION. I QUICKLY DISCOVERED MANY OF MY COWORKERS WERE SPENT. EVEN WORSE. DONE.

"It's not me," a coworker said. "It's this place." The feeling was widespread. Others had also given up wanting to improve, to do better, to create change. They were done caring. Not really—they cared very deeply—yet learned that attempting to put that care into action caused pain. The institution valued physicians and researchers to the point that they could do no wrong, and everyone else existed to serve them. In daily interactions, that mindset meant that non-physicians and non-researchers were treated as interchangeable and expendable. Their work was constantly berated. Everything they did took too long and cost too much, falling short of the unrealistic expectations of the two powerful groups.

Over the years, various groups attempted to rise up and change the environment. "We're professionals," they said. "We do good work. We're tired of being stepped on." When their voices rose, the justifications of the existing culture came just as strongly. They were told that physicians and researchers create income, and other functions were nothing more than a necessary evil and a drain on finances. Budgets were always too low, gratitude didn't exist, and people accepted this state as the organization's chosen way of functioning. The institution's external success offered no incentive to change. It felt like the organization expected employees to say thanks for granting them the privilege of working there! For most employees, the institutional culture was unhealthy, harmful, and disheartening. Yet the organization endured, just as it had for over a century.

How does an organization become so relentlessly toxic? And how do other organizations do the opposite, creating environments where employees thrive? To find answers, we must first understand what culture is.

Common definitions of workplace culture go like this: "Culture is the values, beliefs, and behaviors that define how employees interact." "Culture describes what it's like to work here." "Culture is what happens when the boss isn't around." Edgar Schein, author of *The Corporate Culture Survival Guide*, argues that these definitions oversimplify the complexity of culture. Captions like "the way things get done," "the rites and rituals of a company," and "our values and behaviors" all overlook the core components of culture.

Shein describes three levels of culture: artifacts, espoused values, and underlying assumptions. These distinctions might sound academic, yet they deliver powerful insights.

- **Artifacts** are what you see, hear, and feel when you enter a place. Think of the last restaurant you went to. Was it clean? Were you greeted happily? What was the vibe? Were the host and wait staff friendly and helpful? Did the manager stop by your table? Was the staff engaged? The same questions apply to any organization—a digital agency, manufacturer, school, or city hall. Working hours, dress codes, decision-making processes, and rites and rituals are all types of cultural artifacts.
- **Espoused values** showcase the values a company says they have, compared to the values they live out. For instance, a healthcare company might say they are patient-focused, yet every interaction makes you feel like a number. Or a tech firm claims to be customer-focused, but its applications are difficult to use. Conversely, when a firm knows itself, its espoused values align with how it behaves. Like when a firm that says it strongly values individual insight creates an atmosphere of preparedness, careful internal deliberation, and ample time for employees to think deeply.
- **Underlying assumptions** are expectations left unsaid. A firm

might habitually debate every decision until reaching a unanimous agreement without explicitly teaching this practice to new team members. Newcomers instead experience the environment firsthand and figure out for themselves how things work. Underlying assumptions are often put in place by founders and leaders who find them effective. The values that brought success come to be taken for granted and ingrained. Since success has been achieved, the unstated ideals must be right and therefore are continually reinforced without challenge.

Colin D. Ellis, a culture expert with more energy than anyone I have ever met, passionately helps firms be intentional and successful with their culture. His international work spans books, speaking, podcasts, and coaching organizations to improve their culture.

"Proper work is about creating value, solving problems, and making things better than they were before," he says. "The real question isn't whether today's workers are doing proper work. It's whether today's leaders are creating proper working environments and ensuring managers have the capabilities to uphold them." He adds, "Culture isn't something that happens to us. It's something we choose to build."

THINK AND DISCUSS (PART ONE)

- How would you describe the culture of your past and current employers?
- What are the good aspects of these cultures?
- What are the downsides of these cultures?
- What aspects of the cultures helped you enjoy work?

***Every organization, team, group, and community has a culture.
Culture results from several interrelated factors.***

The basics exist in every workplace—implied or stated. Basics such as mission, vision, values, strategy, and goals. To accomplish these, organizations set up structures, systems, processes, and procedures—documenting how things get done. Layered on top are performance, measurement, errors, and mistakes, and the associated correction systems.

Once those pieces are in place, culture can form. Max De Pree, former chairman of Herman Miller, states in *Leadership Is an Art* that one of his mantras is: "What we believe precedes policy and practice." He advocated that personal and corporate value systems should be aligned—or as closely integrated—as possible. The value system at work should be integrated with the value systems in families, churches, and other groups.

According to Schein, culture focuses on four main areas:

1. **Communication** is how members interact with each other. In person, text, email, group chats, phone calls, and in meetings. The norms that are created, accidentally or with intention, set the expectations of others who join, participate, or interact with the group.
2. **Group boundaries and identity** define who is in and who is out. Do you need a badge at work? Are you a part of the bonus structure? Do you get told secrets?
3. **Authority and relationships** are who is in charge, what they lead, who has power, and how power is wielded. Can you speak your mind? When and where? Are interactions formal or informal?
4. **Reviews, rewards, recognition, and status** are about who gets recognized and why. Who gets promoted? Who gains power?

These four aspects of culture often develop accidentally, with the environment reflecting whoever happens to be in charge at the time.

A division within a large organization, for example, was financially underperforming. The company brought in a new division head tasked with righting the financial ship and getting back to profitability. The culture changes he instituted included holding leaders accountable by publicly screaming at them. He drove results by holding nothing back and going on the attack. Before this leader's arrival, the culture was very much the opposite. This new culture resulted in higher performance and a positive financial result, but the division head was driven out because of toxic behavior. Was that a win for healthy culture? Not really. His departure only happened after he achieved results. The organization chose to look the other way until he achieved his goal, causing deep pain to many people along the way.

When we start to unpack the complexities of culture, we often discover superstar employees who are terrible people. The company applauds their results and overlooks bad behaviors, telling themselves that results are all that matter. The same goes for kiss-up, beat-down management, where mid-level leaders learn that praising their leaders while berating their team members leads to recognition and power. And gossip, rumors, lying, and cheating all may be tolerated if financial performance is achieved.

Colin D. Ellis wrote an entire book on this phenomenon. *Detox Your Culture* warns of the damage created by unhealthy cultures. He notes that toxic workplaces display one or more of the following elements:

- Bullying
- Racism
- Misogyny
- Homophobia
- Non-inclusive
- Verbal or emotional abuse
- Lack of workforce diversity
- Fear
- Micromanagement
- Harassment
- Sexism
- Employee monitoring
- Pay inequity
- Lack of trust
- Favoritism

Colin's list of toxic elements ranges from obviously visible, tangible behaviors to those that are abstract and tough to see.

Many elements develop unintentionally when Schein's four elements aren't prioritized, measured, and nurtured. In other instances, organizational leaders directly cause or encourage these negative developments. At Uber, for example, leaders intentionally created a working environment embodying many toxic elements. Yet Uber was and continues to be successful despite its destructive founder and subsequent culture.

Given these realities, is improving culture a lost cause? If many companies without an intentional focus on culture can be successful in size, growth, and finances, why bother investing in a culture?

Most organizations make at least a minimal effort in culture, realizing it can help attract talent, retain employees, and prevent turnover. For a time, companies imitated Google by installing office ping pong tables and slides and instituting happy hours and free food meant to keep employees engaged—and physically present. Despite these outward attempts to show care for employees, loyalty to firms has dramatically decreased. A January 2024 report from the US Bureau of Labor Statistics showed average job tenure has fallen to 3.9 years, the lowest since 2002.

Julie had been employed by a firm for several years and was considering leaving. The favoritism towards males, the lack of leadership opportunities for mid-career people like her, and her constant feeling of not being one of the guys caused her to consider switching firms. Then a multi-year project came along, and she was put on the team. The client announced that the size and complexity of the project required all team members from the top five firms working on the project to office together five days a week in a place dedicated to the project, which meant no one on the team was going to work in their own company's office for a very long time.

While this declaration created all kinds of logistical challenges, Julie welcomed it as an opportunity. The outcome would be either a great experience or a complete disaster. As the group set up shop, Julie realized the effort resembled a startup company, an experience she had never been part of. As the most senior person from her firm assigned to the project, Julie called a meeting with the top leaders from the other four firms. She asked one question: What will our culture be?

The five leaders collaborated diligently to answer her question. Each pulled good elements from their current firms, and most noted unhealthy elements they wanted to avoid. Together, they put down on paper their culture goals—what they would do and what they wouldn't. Knowing they would be together for four or five years—and physically distanced from their individual employers—gave them the opportunity to create the culture they wanted.

THINK AND DISCUSS (PART TWO)

- How much are you able to impact the culture where you work—or not?
- What steps could you take to change culture in your workplace?
- How could you determine if culture is moving where you want it to go?
- Is a culture always driven by a person? Can a culture live on when the leader who created it is no longer there?

Culture can be aspirational. And truly healthy culture takes constant effort in a consistent direction.

Many firms express values and behaviors to the outside world that are drastically different from what their employees experience. Sure, the organization says they do these things, but everyone knows they don't. Many firms struggle to prevent toxic elements from taking hold, especially if the organization is successful.

Culture isn't a one-and-done. As legendary basketball coach Phil Jackson stated in his book *Eleven Rings*, "The mistake that championship-winning teams often make is to try to repeat their winning formula." There's no formula, no blueprint to copy and replicate. Humans are complex, and the cultures created take constant effort and energy. And because individuals constantly change, even if the same people are present in an organization, their experiences, desires, focus, wants, and needs continually shift. Once you have a winning culture, something about that culture will surely look different in six months!

Much of what we encounter as culture springs up organically, for better or for worse. What happens to a good culture that has been driven by an individual or a small group? Can culture outlive them when they're gone?

Consider a health care system, where a talented CEO arrived and revamped the organization for the better. Less than a year after the CEO's departure, the place reverted to the old ways. This rubber-band effect seems to be the norm. Plenty of examples show how enterprise-wide culture shifted after the leader left—like Zappos, Uber, and Yahoo, where cultures were torn down and recreated in the vision of new leadership. Microsoft, Apple, and Southwest Airlines have all struggled to maintain their cultures after their founders departed. Nevertheless, it's possible for intentional cultures to survive and indeed thrive beyond individual leaders.

THINK AND DISCUSS (PART THREE)

- How can you and others collaborate to identify the culture you have and the culture you want?
- What can you do to intentionally create culture?

- How can you involve people around you to create a culture?
- How can you measure progress toward a more positive culture?

**With intention and care, people can choose the culture
they want and make it happen.**

After Julie and other leaders wrapped up their highly successful project, they returned to their firms. They brought the wildly successful culture elements into their companies—they were able to share, educate, and shift cultures. Some organizations moderately improved, while others were completely overhauled. Julie found little success showing the benefits of dedicated effort to an intentional culture, meeting roadblock after roadblock. Julie was eventually asked to join a firm that made clear during the hiring process that they wanted her—in fact, they needed her—to bring her dedication to culture to their organization. They recognized her impact on the people within the long-term project and excitedly embraced Julie as a valued culture leader.

The steps to define and set forth culture can be created by any group of people—a project team, department, division, or entire company. Now is the best time to ask yourself this crucial question: How am I helping create a culture today where I and others want to work?

CHAPTER 11

Work-Life Balance

YOU'RE TOO SMART TO PLAN YOUR LIFE AROUND PROMISES OF WORK–LIFE BALANCE THAT SOUND TOO GOOD TO BE TRUE. MAYBE IT WOULD BE PREFERABLE FOR ORGANIZATIONS TO BE BRUTALLY HONEST.

"We here at Corporate, Inc. believe in work–life balance for all our employees. What does that look like? For us, balancing your life in the service of work is the utmost priority. We say your personal life is important, but when the company is on the line, you will balance (i.e., sacrifice) your own life and instead do whatever the company needs. What do we mean by the company being 'on the line'? You'll figure it out eventually, but until then, anytime someone needs something, just do it for the good of the company.

"If you feel like you need to boost your work–life balance, check out our internal website, which offers solutions like 'take a break' and 'find time for yourself.' Applying these insights will help you prepare for the times when you will be required to forego breaks and time for yourself because business is more important than you are as a person. We encourage work–life balance as long as work weighs more when we need it to. In case you need clarification, as an employee of Corporate, Inc., know that balance is a nice concept we pretend to care about. Count on us to give it a tremendous amount of lip service!"

Is this statement real? It sure feels like it, a sense that's reinforced every time a deadline looms. The call comes for all-hands-on-deck, and we give up our personal lives for the company. Or when an important meeting is scheduled outside normal working hours, we're expected to attend because, well, the meeting is important.

THINK AND DISCUSS (PART ONE)

- What's your definition of work–life balance?
- Is work–life balance achievable? Explain.
- To what extent do you achieve work–life balance?
- How does your organization actively help you achieve work–life balance?

Isn't work–life balance a simple math problem? A calculation between the hours we spend at work and the hours we spend on the rest of life trying not to think about work?

That's the time management approach, simplifying work–life balance into the time you spend at one versus the other. Although Ford Motor Company implemented the 40-hour workweek in 1926, the practice was standardized in 1940 with the passage of the Fair Labor Standards Act, which established overtime for anything more than 40 hours a week. In theory, with 168 hours in any given week, if you work 40 hours, you get 128 hours outside work for yourself. If you sleep eight hours each night, that leaves you 72 hours for the life portion of work–life balance. Sounds like the balance tips in favor of life!

Let's break apart the 72 hours of "me time." The average American commutes an hour a day (5 hours), preps meals an hour each day (5 hours), and runs errands and takes care of their household (10 hours per week). Now we're down to 52 hours. Showering, eating, socializing, and other obligations consume considerable time. The amount of actual me time isn't all that great.

And back to the 40-hour work week. How many full-time employees manage to work just 40 hours? They think about work long after they clock out. They talk about it at home. They carry it emotionally and intellectually. They check emails around the clock. The 40-hour workweek isn't quite 40 hours, is it?

Enter the attention dilemma. Alastair Benn states, "We have not lost our ability to focus, we're just focusing on the wrong things—an attention dilemma that has haunted western thought for centuries."

Benn points out that the amount of information thrown at us each day has increased steadily since the founding of the United States. Technology has increased the volume of things we consume, and we continue to struggle with the ability to focus, work deeply, and pay attention. On the job, we constantly shift gears from one task, conversation, meeting, and deadline to the next. Because of the constant brain shifts, we often pay attention only halfway—at best. Then we go home and halfway pay attention to that world. And because we half-work at work, we make up for it by half-working at home. Work–life balance? Impossible!

It turns out our work–life balance can't be simplified into a binary equation. Additionally, the concept can't be viewed as a bad/good balance—that work is bad, and life is good. However, our collective low engagement at work signals that many of us believe that work–life balance is that simple.

Gallup has shown for decades that the average engagement level in America hovers around 33%, meaning that only one out of three people is truly absorbed in the duties of their jobs. The rest of the workforce is at some level checked out. They do what's required and no more. They don't go above and beyond. They see the job as a job, a means to a paycheck. By minimizing time doing bad things (work), we can maximize time doing good things (not work) and thereby achieve work–life balance.

On the surface, this approach can sound appealing. Isn't it enviable that folks can leave work at work and never give another thought to their job once they exit the workplace? But there's a flip slide. Spending 40 hours a week at a job that isn't personally fulfilling isn't a bargain most people can stick with for very long.

The idea of work–life balance showed up in the 1970s, when men were no longer the primary workforce. With men and women alike working, two-income households took hold, and the shift meant both adults needed to juggle family responsibilities. Hence, the birth of "work–life balance." Societal pressures for equal labor opportunities and conditions, plus changing attitudes toward gender roles, resulted in attention to equity.

The circle formed: Work to take care of your family, then go home and take care of your family by investing time in them. But life split in two parts became a conundrum—if you don't build your career, you can't take care of your family. And increasing your time with family means you can't build a career. Something must give, and work–life balance becomes impossible.

Yet for all the talk about culture, workplace wellbeing, and work–life balance, the pressure for a solution grows:

- Technology continues to increase work pressure with constant communications.
- Deadlines continue to compress.
- Expected response times continue to reduce (I emailed you an hour ago, why haven't you responded?).
- Excessive customer service continues to be the norm (Instant gratification, please!).

This is the plague of everyday life.

A work meeting was scheduled for 7 AM, the time I sat down for breakfast with my kids most days. Because we ate breakfast together quite often, I felt okay missing this ritual from time to time. As the day approached, the meeting was switched to the evening. 6 PM. Smack in the middle of an evening of three kids in multiple sports and activities. With my high value of volunteering as a parent, it created a serious conflict. Another team member, also expected to be on the call, needed to care for a family member with a medical procedure scheduled for that evening.

As we sought to reschedule the meeting around these two conflicts, we received a stern no. When we asked for a day to juggle multiple priorities and rearrange schedules, I got a blunt text message. "I need to know right now if you and your colleague will be at this meeting." The point was clear. When push comes to shove, work–life balance isn't important. Our presence wasn't requested. We were told to attend this meeting and ditch our family obligations.

This happens every day, all day, throughout the world. Corporate, Inc. says they want work–life balance, but not at the expense of work. Your life outside work matters less than your job responsibilities.

Is it all gloom and doom? Absolutely not. At least we know what the utopia of work–life balance could look like—the ability to shift on the fly at all times as needed to give undivided attention to the task at hand or to the person in front of you. That would require personal control and autonomy over the demands for your time and attention at work, home, personally, spiritually, and physically. You would take charge of devoting the amount of energy into each calling as you deem necessary.

THINK AND DISCUSS (PART TWO)

- Who do you look up to who has a good work–life balance?
- What does your organization do to promote work–life balance?
- If work–life balance meant undivided attention at whatever you are doing, can you provide undivided attention to your current task at hand—or to the person in front of you?
- To what degree do you have autonomy over the demands of your various roles and your ability to meet these demands?

How can you achieve work–life balance?
Let's start with two simple approaches. You could
1) set strict boundaries, or 2) carve out personal time.

For the sake of this exercise, let's say "strict boundaries" look something like 9–5 with no work outside those hours. Is that possible? Or desirable?

You might assume a leader has the power to achieve work–life balance. While power indeed may exist, take a close look at their lives. Beyond their organizational and financial success. Do they have strong relationships at home? Do they lead healthy lives? Do they work 9–5 and take vacations? Most "successful" people in leadership positions who claim they take vacations and personal time never do. Many leaders model workaholic behavior and expect the same of their employees, at least in seasons of high work demands.

Even if work–life balance isn't a complete mirage, it's also incredibly complicated. Why?

- **Societal focus on materialism, money, and power.** The constant pressure of media, social media, social networks, friends, and family to do more, get more, and be more often places tremendous value on work, work, and more work. We create belief systems that reinforce the idea that sacrificing our lives for work is necessary, acceptable, and even desirable.

- **People must be responsible for their own lives.** The victim mentality is an attractive option. Others keep me down. They're the reason I don't succeed. My life is what it is because my boss, spouse, parents, and teachers prevent me from achieving my potential. I would like to take responsibility for myself, but they won't let me.
- **People must be allowed to set their own boundaries.** Schedules, what we work on, where we work, how we work—when people are empowered with some degree of choice, engagement skyrockets. That's a difficult fact for many leaders to accept and apply.
- **Little changes in one area of life can wreak havoc in other areas.** Signing up for a class sounds easy. Just commit to do it. Yet it often shuts out other parts of life that need your attention at the same time. The same goes for putting and keeping vacation time on the calendar. Or growing a family, taking care of loved ones, and being a part of a community.
- **Achieving work–life balance takes a long time.** Attending a seminar, watching a video, or reading a book won't get you to work–life balance. Finding the rhythm of intentional work–life balance takes effort, energy, and most importantly, time.

What about carving out time for yourself in a quest for work–life balance? That has promise. But it will be forever out of reach if you're stuck in a work-equals-misery mindset. Authentic work–life balance is achieved when you love parts of what you do at work and love the other parts of your life. If you love your work—or most of it—then it's not an intolerable way to spend your day. And it's relatively easy to be 100% present in your work. If that's not the case, you might be physically present, but you're mentally somewhere else. And when you're mentally disengaged, you aren't performing at your best. In the end, that's self-defeating. It negatively impacts you and everyone around you.

As Mike McMullen of Forbes states, "If you aren't living well—taking care of yourself, making healthy choices, and putting your all into work—then it won't matter if your career and personal life are 'balanced.'"

THINK AND DISCUSS (PART THREE)

- What are your non-negotiables for self-care, even when you get busy?
- How do you set boundaries between work and personal time?
- Do you feel satisfied and have the necessary resources to function at your best in everything you do?
- Are you doing work that fulfills you? How do you know?

To find our way through all the complexities of achieving work–life balance, we must look at ourselves and ask if we're meeting our responsibilities in ways that satisfy us.

Many organizations that embraced the remote work paradigm during 2020 and 2021 subsequently slowly walked back the flexibility of remote work by making unilateral and demanding return-to-office policies. Companies such as Amazon, Tesla, and JPMorgan Chase have created environments with significant hindrances to work–life balance.

Ashley took a consulting position with a large banking organization, with the understanding that the position would be hybrid at the start and transition to completely remote work. When the CEO announced sweeping changes to the remote and hybrid working arrangements—no more remote work, everyone back in the office full time—Ashley shared the human impact of this broad sweeping policy change.

"For me, remote work wasn't merely about convenience. It was about maintaining vital connections with my family, particularly my grandparents in Delaware. The ability to seamlessly transition between New York and Delaware was essential to my life.

The lack of support from my colleagues was undeniable. I exhausted my vacation days (not personal leave, vacation days) to be with my grandmother, only to receive an email from a coworker demanding I complete my work during this time off.

When corporate leaders make sweeping declarations about ending remote work, I wonder if they have considered the human cost. Do these mandates come with provisions for childcare expenses? Transportation costs? Additional paid leave for family emergencies? The privilege of making such unilateral decisions affecting thousands of lives carries with it a responsibility to consider their real-world implications.

These aren't just policy changes. They're decisions that ripple through families, alter life trajectories, and sometimes force impossible choices between professional obligations and irreplaceable personal moments.

As companies continue to shape the future of work, I hope they remember that behind every policy decision are thousands of personal stories like mine—stories of people trying their best to balance their responsibilities to both their careers and their loved ones."

To achieve balance in our current world, remote, hybrid, and other creative work arrangements aren't a luxury. They're required in our complex world.

Balance is misleading. Because life constantly changes, the balance will shift throughout your life. At times, the balance will be weighed toward work, and at other times toward personal needs. The idea of achieving work–life balance can imply that the journey has a final destination. Will you get there?

I hope not. This is a journey we need to pursue throughout our lives. The reflection required by the journey allows us to pause, understand, acknowledge, and proceed with intentionality. Through consistent self-evaluation and self-awareness, we can find our own definition of work–life balance and find ways to live out what it means to each of us.

CHAPTER 12

Creativity

WHAT HAPPENS IF A TEAM OF EXPERTS IS GIVEN THE FREEDOM TO EXPLORE ALTERNATIVES TO ACCEPTED NORMS AND PRACTICES? CREATIVITY IN ACTION!

To fulfill its mission of providing healthcare to a grossly underserved community, a hospital needed a state-of-the-art operating room. For each day that passed without the new operating room, people suffered from a lack of specialized technology. With lives at stake, speed was everything, yet building an OR is always a complex, lengthy process.

Enter a team with combined design and construction experience totaling hundreds of years. Going super-fast shouldn't be a problem. But how?

The team huddled and determined that the standard process would require fourteen months. Hospital leadership asked if the project could go faster. What if money was unlimited? How long would the project take? Sure, the hospital could throw money at the project, but the team could still only physically put so many workers on the worksite at the same time. The team considered skipping reviews, quality checks, and other standard process steps, only to discover that this extreme maneuvering would make little impact on project duration.

Then an architect asked, "What if we throw out our entire process?"

The typical design process starts with drawings—architects sketch concepts, ask the people who will work the room for feedback—draw again—get more input—repeat over and over until a design is finalized and approved. Engineers and detailers then painstakingly draw every square inch of the area. Then they submit to a state or city office to obtain a building permit, a process that takes many months.

This project needed an entirely different approach that could drive the design much faster. The architect who advocated throwing out the usual process proposed that the team skip the drawing phase and instead create a physical space the same size as the planned operating room. The team found an unused space in the hospital, roughly the same size as the new operating room, and quickly got to work. They taped lines on the floor, rolled in an operating table, and outfitted the room with standard equipment. They invited surgery teams to perform mock operations. With each trial, the surgery teams provided feedback, the "fake" room was adjusted, and the level of detail grew. The team added walls constructed from cardboard, the amount of equipment expanded, and cabinets were mocked up using foam, all without a single drawing. After three weeks, the team had a room made of cardboard, foam, and duct tape that met the needs of the surgery teams. All of which was bought into by the surgery team. Design complete!

Then, engineers and detailers went to work, and in less than two weeks, they produced drawings ready to submit for a permit. A six-month design process had been compressed to five weeks. As the permit review got underway, the construction team continued to plan how to execute the project. Being able to move around inside a life-size model greatly simplified developing a specific work plan. The team brought in all the builders, and just like the surgery teams, the tradespeople practiced how they would construct the room step by step.

This was creativity in action!

THINK AND DISCUSS (PART ONE)

- What does creativity look like to you?
- How does creativity show up in your day? Your week?
- When was the last time you felt you were able to be creative?
- Where do you feel you are most creative?

Are all people able to be creative? What's the difference between those who seem to easily create and those who struggle?

Creativity isn't a rare ability or talent. In fact, creativity is fundamental to being human. Yet why do some people seem to have a natural aptitude that others lack?

Let's consider what it means to be creative.

Tangible creative acts, such as writing music, painting a picture, or writing a book, are good examples of creativity in action. Each creation requires some degree of talent, and none happens without significant work, time, and energy. And there's a knowable pattern of how that happens.

My youngest son, for example, enjoys computer games, and one of his favorites involves building rollercoasters and theme parks. His creativity shines when he builds new rides. At first, I cringed at his creations, mostly because, as an eight-year-old, he had no concept of physics and g-forces. He didn't fully process the mock deaths in the game that ensued when animated humans flew off the rails because of faulty designs.

Sometimes I got sick watching his rides operate. Yet as my son grew, so did his designs. They became more complex. He studied videos, visited real-life theme parks, and absorbed the world around him by gathering input, observing, listening, practicing, and watching. His mind cataloged mountains of data. He gradually incorporated various pieces and parts of that data into his designs. He added scenery. He began to understand how a story during a ride can impact the experience.

Games like the one my son enjoys absolutely engage creativity, as does playing an instrument, woodworking, model building, tending a garden, and a million other activities in life.

Why is it important for us to be creative?

Harvard Business School states several benefits of creativity on the job:

- **Creativity accompanies innovation.** Innovation is improvement, either through a novel invention or by eliminating unnecessary process steps. Innovation makes creativity real and effective. Innovation asks the question "Is it useful?"
- **Creativity can increase productivity.** Yes, the start of a creative engagement decreases productivity. The search for improvement requires pushing, bending, and occasionally tossing out routines,

procedures, and structures, all of which burn time. Though searching for a better way ultimately accelerates output.

- **Creativity may force adaptability.** Large organizations typically develop a low tolerance for risk, and their success proves they know how to do things. When markets and employees need change, organizations often struggle to adapt. Encouraging creativity supports initiatives in environments where resistance is the natural reaction to change.
- **Creativity is often necessary for growth.** Fast-growing firms create and scale solutions as quickly as possible before competitors appear. Once competition is present, their solution is no longer unique, requiring the firm to lower prices or further refine solutions to continue to grow. Or they might find new markets. Or create additional first-of-a-kind solutions. Replicating the past is rarely the answer, and creativity can rapidly open paths overlooked by structured thinking.

How do we jumpstart creativity? How can we determine where our attempts at creativity would be worth our investment of time, effort, and money?

Traditional management philosophy approaches problems from the top down. A leader looks at the situation—such as an assembly line, written process, or coding structure—studies it, then dictates that workers should implement a new solution developed by the leader. When the quality movement appeared in the 1980s, however, people had a better idea. If a process requires improvement, ask the people who do the work. Give them the opportunity to improve how things get done. Ask them how they would do things differently and what they need to make it happen.

Note that creativity isn't always desirable. If a plane is supposed to take you from point A to point B, you don't want pilots to be creative and test whether the plane can do a barrel roll. And you don't want the surgeon doing a routine knee replacement deciding to experiment on you. Those types of situations aside, where could we bring creativity to our work?

THINK AND DISCUSS (PART TWO)

- Are you able to be creative at work? Where, when, and why—or not?
- Are you allowed to schedule time to explore creative options?
- Where do you find inspiration for creativity?
- When have you tried to be creative but got stuck? How did you get unstuck? Or did you have to let the idea go?

Sooner or later, we all get stopped cold in the creative process, and the experience might convince us we lack creativity. But there are proven processes we can learn and adapt to our efforts.

Rick Rubin, music producer for Run DMC, the Beastie Boys, and LL Cool J, and one of Time's 100 Most Influential People in the world, shared his version of the creative process in his book The Creative Act: A Way of Being. He states the creative process is four parts: seeds, experimentation, crafting, and completion.

1. **Seeds:** "We're searching for potential starting points that, with love and care, can grow into something beautiful."
2. **Experimentation:** "We play with different combinations and possibilities to see if any of them reveal how the seed wants to develop."
3. **Crafting:** "We need to look away from the open field and turn towards a winding staircase a hundred stories tall. A long, precarious climb lies ahead." Crafting is the laborious part of creativity.
4. **Completion:** "We leave behind discovery and building. With a beautiful volume of material crafted before us, the final form is refined to be released into the world."

My son follows this four-part process as he designs, builds, and runs rollercoasters. He **seeds** by studying different types of coasters, researching, watching videos, and visiting real parks. The seeds form in his mind. While some "ah-has!" never become true seeds, others take shape and begin to form an idea. Then he **experiments** with different elements, types, speeds, and more. Once he has a good feeling for the pieces and parts available, the hard part begins—**crafting**, which is time-consuming, labor-intensive, and at times, tedious. He mostly enjoys the many hours he puts into a single ride.

Then comes **completion**, usually announced with "Dad! You have to come see this!"

Those are the best creative journeys. On many of his journeys, he gets stuck. He's unsure which roller coaster type to use—launched versus chain lift versus inverted. Or he doesn't quite grasp how physics impacts the ride—like if the train takes the tight curve at 90 mph, why do people fly out? At that point, the crafting portion loses gas. Inspiration feels like it's vanished. He can't see where he wants to go, and the hardest part is when he finishes a section only to go back and redo it. Again. And again. And again.

We assume that music artists and other "creatives" pump out hits without problems. Why can't we produce great things creatively all the time in our areas of expertise? We should learn from the fact that even the most successful creators get stuck. Rick Rubin explains multiple ways he helps artists get unstuck:

- **Small steps.** Break your work into the smallest possible measure of progress as a means for getting traction. If you're a writer and feel blocked, try writing one sentence every day. Or 500 words a day about anything at all.
- **Change your environment.** Shake up the environment where you create. Go somewhere new, rearrange your furniture, or play with lighting.
- **Change the stakes.** Imagine this moment is the last time you will ever paint again. Then paint.
- **Alter the perspective.** Change how you look at things. Double the font on the pages you're reviewing. Or amp up the sound of the song you're listening to.
- **Play with imagery.** Add visuals to your work that normally don't need graphics. See if that rocks your mind.

Does creativity succeed all the time? No. Otherwise, there wouldn't be countless unfinished symphonies, paintings, books, process improvements, designs, and projects that died before completion.

Many dead ends are the result of losing energy during the crafting stage. How might that reality play out in an organization with low risk tolerance?

Paul strongly believed his organization was wasting huge money processing orders. The cost of paper involved ran into thousands of dollars. Add in all the manual processing, from filling out forms to hand routing copies to requiring multiple personal signatures on every order. Paul's team alone processed more than ten thousand orders a year, and there were multiple teams just like Paul's!

Paul worked with a small group to streamline the process. He knew better than to ask permission at a firm that was over a hundred years old, profitable, and entrenched in habits. Knowing the firm was very numbers-focused, he believed the organization would adopt any alternative process that saved millions.

His team worked tirelessly in secret and outside normal working hours. At first, it was fun. Seed ideas were tossed around, and experiments ran fast. Secrecy added to the importance and excitement.

As the weeks passed, doubt crept in. What if someone finds out? What if we get in trouble? Could we be fired over this? The initial high of the creative process was slowly ground to dust by company culture. Stability, consistency, reliability, and adherence to process were valued. Not secret late-night meetings. One by one, the team members dropped off. Eventually, Paul had to face facts and put aside his own creative impulse.

Paul's experience did teach him one thing. He's very good at experimenting. Although he really wants to drive a creative process to completion, he found his groove experimenting. The fast pace, quick hits, and even the lessons he drew from failures gave him a rush. An idea that didn't work just meant he got to try again, some other way. He noticed, however, that his colleagues weren't as comfortable with this phase of creative efforts. Certain people preferred to just get things done. When Paul was enjoying playing and testing, his colleagues, who preferred to wrap things up, anxiously awaited the results of his experiments so they could drive something to completion.

Most of us naturally prefer one of the phases of creativity—to create seed, experiment, craft, or finish. The key is to know our preferences and embrace the fact that creativity requires effort in each. Quickly moving to finish robs time from experiments that could make the work even better. And staying in the experimental stage too long prevents others from enjoying the fruits of the labor.

THINK AND DISCUSS (PART THREE)

- Are you an experimenter—or a finisher? What's your evidence?
- How does creativity make us better people?
- How do you encourage creativity in yourself? Others? Groups?
- Where can you help others be more creative at work or in life?

> *A creative environment requires intentionality. When people are given objectives and then set loose to creatively find their way forward, great results happen.*

When Val joined a new firm, she was thrust into crafting proposals and delivering sales pitches. In her industry, there were established standards for both. The written proposals were formal, and with a multi-year track record of obtaining millions of dollars of work, the firm had a well-documented process. Likewise, the process for sales pitches was determined by the history of winning and not winning millions of dollars of work. Although Val understood this one-size-fits-all approach, she was also in tune with the people she was prospecting and thought creativity would drive even better results.

Val was instructed to go win the work. She knew the prospects team well and immediately suggested that written proposals be cut from several dozen pages to six. Then she challenged the practice of formal sales pitches, which were always a scripted slide show. Her knowledge of prospects and her own people told her the sales pitch would be better delivered and received if it were structured as a work session. Instead of telling a prospect what they would do, they would jump in and do what they do best—partnering with the client to figure things out collaboratively!

Val's approach could have been met with enormous internal resistance. In some settings, it might even get her fired. Yet Val had sown the seeds of recreating sales delivery for years, and she chose a firm that set goals and allowed salespeople to inject their own creativity to get results. Val knew what she was doing when she helped her delivery team experiment with a variety of alternatives for the written piece and sales pitch. Once the team agreed on an approach that they all felt would be relevant and effective, then they labored to craft their document and presentation. As the due date neared, Val and her team locked in and finalized their work. They completed and delivered.

The creative atmosphere created by her firm—providing a clear goal coupled with trusting a leader and her team—followed Rick Rubin's creative approach of seeds, experiment, labor, and completion. Val's approach fit her, her team, and the prospect, and they repeated the process in future pursuits with tremendous success.

As Rubin says, "Living life as an artist is a practice. You are either engaging in the practice or you're not. It makes no sense to say you're not good at it. It's like saying, 'I'm not good at being a monk.' You are either living as a monk or you're not. We tend to think of the artist's work as the output. The real work of the artist is a way of being in the world."

Creativity is a skill we all have as human beings. When we understand the process and seek an environment that allows us to work in each of the four stages, each and every one of us can create.

CHAPTER 13

Empowerment

EVEN THE MOST COMPETENT INDIVIDUAL HAS LIMITS TO WHAT THEY CAN DO ALONE. WHEN WE MAKE OURSELVES THE HUB OF INFORMATION AND DECISIONS, WE LIMIT WHAT OTHERS CAN ACCOMPLISH.

Pete was a project manager at a large corporation consistently ranked as an employer of choice. In this prized role, he was assigned to his largest project ever. He needed to direct numerous stakeholders, including the client, several departments within his own organization, and dozens of external vendors. His weekly meetings regularly involved 20 or 30 participants and lasted for hours. He dealt with an astounding volume of communication via email, calls, and in-person conversations. Pete did his job well, but no one person could stay on top of every aspect of every project. Yet that's exactly what everyone expected of Pete. And up until now, this structure worked. Sort of.

Internal and external team members all regarded Pete as their leader, and for his part, Pete aimed for total awareness. He wanted to control every detail. Because vendors knew Pete controlled the client's assessment of their performance, they went along with Pete's constant oversight. Susie was one of those vendors, and early in her career, she learned to include the project manager on everything—emails, phone calls, any and all information that was pertinent to the project; she knew to always include Pete. While Susie often made recommendations to the client, she never acted without Pete's direct approval. And she would never think of talking to other project members without going through Pete.

Pete had a problem. Many dozens of project team members thought exactly like Susie. Everyone copied him on emails, sought his approval for decisions, and expected him to act as go-between. Given the scale of Pete's projects, his inbox was always overflowing, and he couldn't keep up. Frustrated, he sent an email to the entire project team—everyone he could think of, internal and external—which said:

> *You all must stop copying me on every email. If you have a question or need a discussion with another project team member, go to that person, ask your question directly, and have the discussion. I do NOT need to be involved in everything. If you expect an answer from me, more likely than not, I don't know and need to ask someone. So just skip me and ask directly. You are all adults, you are all professionals, and you are all allowed to talk to each other without me. If you involve me, I will either give you the wrong answer or slow you down trying to find the right answer. Just figure it out and bring the remaining questions and decisions to our project meetings.*

At first, many of the project team members weren't sure what the email meant. Was Pete mad? Had they done something wrong? At the next project team meeting, Pete read his email out loud word for word. He wanted to make clear that he indeed meant what he said. Yes, he was frustrated. More importantly, he was learning that his job as project manager wasn't to control the flow of information or make routine decisions. It was to empower his team. The first step in that direction was giving them permission to talk to each other without him mediating. They could reach out to each other without fear.

THINK AND DISCUSS (PART ONE)

- What is empowerment?
- Where are you empowered at work?
- Where are you empowered in your life?
- How does it feel to be empowered?

Empowerment isn't limited to the workplace. It's the dynamic behind many powerful inspirational stories that capture our hearts and minds.

It's hard not to love hearing about someone empowered to take charge and accomplish a feat that felt unlikely, if not impossible. But what does empowerment mean? Consider the definitions:

1. Empowerment is people having power and control over their own lives.
2. Empowerment is the process of gaining freedom and power to do what you want and to control what happens.
3. Empowerment is the capacity of individuals, groups, or communities to take control of their circumstances, exercise power, and achieve their own goals. It's the process by which, individually and collectively, they can help themselves and others to maximize the quality of their lives.

Having power over our destiny is an essential element of empowerment. This is fundamental to our well-being and success as individuals. Think of the person who goes through life feeling oppressed, stuck, victimized, and hopeless. Then something or someone inspires them to believe their life doesn't have to be that way. Internally, that person feels a surge of will. They have the power to alter the course of their life and exercise control over what previously felt beyond reach.

Take Cheryl, a parent who felt that the school system wasn't helping her kids. Of her three kids, two were outside the norm. One was extremely gifted, and the other struggled mightily. The school system they attended was overcrowded, understaffed, and poorly funded. That result was an education aligned primarily to kids closer to the middle, which left Cheryl's kids out of luck. Year after year, Cheryl watched her children struggle. The gifted one was bored, and the one with challenges barely passed. While she felt bad, she also believed there was nothing she could do. Then a friend told her about a group of parents in similar situations who were looking for answers. Cheryl suddenly felt less alone, and a glimmer of hope formed inside her. If others were experiencing what she was, then maybe she didn't have to just accept the situation. She could do something.

Or consider Ed's journey. At forty, a horrible car accident cost him his legs. As a lifelong runner, cyclist, and swimmer, he suddenly found himself experiencing what felt like a total loss. He could continue doing his job, but what about his activities—and his community outside work? He ran with friends, cycled in the summers with a local club, and raced with a Masters swimming group. Now he couldn't do any of that. Months of rehab lay ahead of him just to be able to function. Being in and out of the hospital for weeks, plus countless visits to doctors and specialists, sucked the life out of him. As Ed was thrust into a new world, he slowly made connections with others experiencing all sorts of challenges. Whether those challenges resulted from accidents or were present since birth, many he met were, like him, at a loss for hope. However, he found others who had managed not just to survive but thrive. He was able to wrestle his way back to hope and empowered himself. Before long, he was competing in all sorts of races again.

Empowerment can be found inside a person. Rather than feeling scared and alone, drifting along as a victim of circumstance, people who feel empowered take charge. They look for areas they can control. They pay attention and listen intently to the world around them. They take action on small points.

What causes people like Cheryl and Ed to move from hopelessness to empowerment? Is it environmental? Spiritual? The people they surround themselves with? How they choose to spend their time? What moves someone to action, whether in an instant or over time?

THINK AND DISCUSS (PART TWO)

- Where have you seen or heard stories of empowerment in action in your community, work, or individual lives?
- Is empowerment internal and/or external?
- What factors need to exist to possess a sense of empowerment?
- Why is empowerment important?

Empowerment at work gets complicated. Sure, the rewards might be high. But the risks of empowering people can feel higher.

You can empower a high school student to create a presentation and teach a seminar. If they fail, so what? They'll learn from the experience. And attendees might be bored. Who cares? But what happens when you empower a team member or direct report, and they crash and burn?

You might feel the possibility is cringeworthy. But it won't happen. As their manager, you would ensure they're prepared, good to go, with no chance of failure. In fact, you would have the person so dialed in that they can't help but hit it out of the park.

How can you be so sure? Because you're more invested in their success than they are.

Wait a second. Think about that. Did you really empower them? If empowerment is about giving up control, then it doesn't sound like you let them struggle enough that the success was truly their own. Quite the opposite. In fact, it might make you wonder if you can truly empower people at work if it means giving up control.

There are small steps you can take to empower people at work. How about allowing them to flex their work hours if appropriate for the position and tasks? Or how about letting them decide how they dress for the workplace—they are adults, aren't they? These simple steps demonstrate trust and allow people a sense of control. Remember, the definitions state empowerment is gaining freedom and power to do what you want or to control what happens. This won't happen in every aspect at work, because there are some rules and regulations we all must follow for businesses to function.

Now consider areas where people could gain even more significant control. Here's one that could revolutionize your workplace: Do employees feel empowered to say no to their boss, leader, or manager? How could you help make that happen?

Jim's team oversaw maintenance at a large facility. With a 24/7 operation under their care, his team was always present, keeping the lights on and making critical repairs. Unforeseen, Jim was called away for two weeks with little notice. He let his team know he would be out of contact for that time, and it was up to them to keep the place operating. When Jim returned, he wasn't surprised to find everything humming along just as well as when he left.

How did this happen? What was Jim's magic? Did he craft a big announcement that he was suddenly empowering his team? No. He spent years developing his people. He listened to their suggestions. He let them make decisions, telling them to only bring him the stuff they couldn't resolve. Even then, he habitually pushed them to start the conversation by sharing their best thinking on addressing the situation. By celebrating his team's ability to get work done using their own skills and experience, he demonstrated trust.

When Jim was suddenly removed from the environment, the culture of empowerment that Jim had cultivated meant that team members already felt they had the power to take charge in his absence.

Empowering people requires a culture that is clear, articulated, and cared for. If culture happens by accident, it's a gamble to empower people.

Take Ryan and his team. Ryan felt that he had good values and a good culture. Work got done, people stayed with the organization, and he was confident his team was full of decent people. Sure, they had corporate values and other propaganda on the walls, but that wasn't necessary to get the work done. They were a solid team. He just felt it.

When his team was tasked with a major project with a lot of risk if they failed, he knew his team would step up. They worked hard for months. Although the schedule continued to slip, the team marched on, telling themselves they would make up the lost time. It was no big deal. They had this. As the project completion date drew closer, a team member emailed everyone on the project. The note was blunt. With three months to go, everyone needed to put in overtime during the week and probably on weekends to meet the deadline. Plan for it. Rearrange your schedules. This is expected.

As Ryan read the note, his first thought was Good! The team is coming together to deliver. Then he thought again. He wondered if he had created this crisis. He had enabled a culture where crunch times happened, and people were expected to abandon their personal lives for the sake of work. Missed kid games, less sleep, poorer eating habits, and skipped workouts were all expected when work was on the line. Once the project was done, would anyone say the trade-offs were worth it? Is this what he wanted?

While Ryan thought he had empowered his team to make decisions, he accidentally allowed the culture to create itself. Had he been intentional about culture, perhaps he would have set values and behavioral expectations. He could have communicated that, as a team, work–life balance is non-negotiable. That expectation may have pushed the team to stay true to that value earlier in the project and prevent work from falling behind. Could Ryan have been more hands-on, provided tighter oversight, or established a higher level of communication with his team? Yes, yes, and yes—though one needs to consider the impacts and ramifications of each approach. Remember, we're talking about empowerment: How could Ryan have empowered his team in a way that changed the result?

THINK AND DISCUSS (PART THREE)

- Where is empowerment good? When is it not so good?
- How do you create empowerment in others?
- What does it look like to empower people who mess up? How does it feel?
- Who are you empowering today? How?

The Internet is full of wonderful and mighty one-liners that, on the surface, feel warm and fuzzy.

But if you think harder, the meanings often turn out to be so wide that applying them can have both positive and negative impacts. I believe empowerment is a strong positive. I also recognize it takes real intent accompanied by hard work.

Take a quote by John Maxwell, one of the greatest business minds. He says, "Leaders become great, not because of their power, but because of their ability to empower others." This quote is powerful. It rings true. Think of how many leaders have shared this view, only to have it challenged when their success is on the line. When a leader is personally at risk, a sudden urge of self-protection and self-preservation can cause them to rip away the empowerment they have given. That's tragic.

Every few years, empowerment becomes a hot business topic. It seems to rise and fall with the willingness of top leaders to risk letting employees do the jobs they were hired to do. It gains popularity when business is good and recedes when business trends downward. That's when command-and-control regains popularity.

Empowering yourself is an amazing journey. Empowering others is just as amazing—if not more so. When you truly seek to empower others at work, with family, among friends, or in any group, your commitment and sense of purpose can help everyone feel the joy real empowerment brings.

CHAPTER 14

———

Courage

YOU TOOK A RISK, INCHED OUT ON A LIMB, AND MADE THE LEAP. BUT YOU WERE TERRIFIED THE ENTIRE TIME. DOES THAT STILL COUNT AS COURAGE?

My youngest son joined me on a mid-summer business trip to Houston. We had an afternoon open, so we searched together online for something to do. We spotted a sizable downtown park offering kayak rentals, though the outfitter wouldn't be open during our visit. After studying alternative activities, my son kept coming back to kayaking. We expanded our search and found rentals available on the bayou outside the city. I booked a tandem kayak.

We would meet in a parking lot with a boat launch. This wasn't my first rental rodeo, so I expected a small crowd of other renters and a truck hauling a trailer stacked with boats. A guide would set us up, give us a safety talk, then send us off to explore. As we waited, a guy in a white pickup pulled up with a lone kayak jutting out the back. The company logo on the truck was a giveaway that he was our guide. When I walked over and introduced myself, he nodded toward our kayak and said we were the only ones heading out that afternoon. He would be back in three hours to pick us up. We strapped on our life jackets and put our water bottles in the boat. The guy gave me a map and showed me a few good places to go. As we settled onto the kayak, he said, "If you see any alligators, give them plenty of space. They won't bother you."

I'm from Chicago. I don't hang out with alligators. I thought he was kidding. No, he assured me, there really are gators. Big ones. Like 20 feet long. He pushed us away from shore and said, "Have fun!"

My paddle disappeared into the muddy brown water as my eleven-year-old son happily perched in the front of our sit-on-top kayak, a giant hunk of injection-molded plastic with a couple of humps for seats. Lacking was even the minimal sense of protection from tucking inside a traditional kayak. I instantly recalled childhood encounters with alligators at Chicago's Lincoln Park Zoo. In the basement of the reptile building, behind thick glass, a half dozen giant gators lay in wait, eyes and nostrils above the water, clearly wanting to eat me. I was six or seven at the time, and as an adult, I projected that vision onto the bayou. With every push of the paddle deeper into the bayou, my mental freak-out grew worse.

THINK AND DISCUSS (PART ONE)

- How do you define courage?
- What examples and stories of courage can you share?
- When have you been courageous? How did that turn out?
- How are courage and fear related?

Some days our fears feel strong inside us. Other days we feel like we can conquer any challenge the day might bring. Is fear a necessary element of courage?

Consider these definitions of courage:

1. The ability to do something that frightens us.
2. Strength in the face of pain or grief.
3. The choice to confront agony, pain, danger, uncertainty, or intimidation.

And look at these definitions of fear:
1. An unpleasant emotion caused by the belief that someone or something is dangerous, likely to cause pain, or a threat.
2. Be afraid of (someone or something) as likely to be dangerous, painful, or threatening.

It seems like courage, by definition, is a response to some degree of distress. Worries about losing our jobs, getting hurt, failing, looking stupid—all these worries exist in us. But is true fear always present? That depends on factors like culture, environment, mood, and our mental, physical, and emotional state.

Recall times you built up the courage to do something. You stepped up and out, and you hit a home run. Your courage produced great things. "Great," according to your definition, of course. The great things may have been small to others, but to you they were amazing!

Or is it easier to think of examples where you were courageous yet fell short of your expectations? Or downright failed? Were you courageous even if you were shot down?

Think deeper about your personal examples of being courageous. Who were you courageous with? A family member? A boss? A stranger? A thing—like a goal or activity? In each example, did you need to work up courage, or did it come in a flash of bravery at just the right moment?

In the bayou, my fear ran high. The thought that an alligator could pop out of the murk at any moment nearly had me nearly physically paralyzed. My mental movie of horrible probabilities was on overdrive. Within a few minutes into the paddle, my son was obviously having a good time, and his courage caught me off guard. Admittedly, he didn't have my vast experience with predatory animals. (Note: I have exactly zero experience with predatory animals.) But my mind was consumed by fear. I didn't expect to spend a playful afternoon worrying about large reptiles attacking us. I needed to rid myself of that feeling—and quickly—because I wasn't about to back out of our kayaking adventure.

That afternoon, I never got to a moment of feeling what I would consider courage. The best I could manage was not letting my boy see my agony.

THINK AND DISCUSS (PART TWO)

- What people do you find it easy—or hard—to be courageous with? Peers, direct reports, your boss, leaders, family, friends, strangers? Why?
- How are professional and personal courage the same? Different?
- Can you find courage in the moment, or do you need time to work up to it?

- What risks come with being courageous? With not being courageous?

Courage comes in various forms because fear is different for everyone. Giving a presentation to a few coworkers can be just as terrifying as dangling on a rappelling rope over the edge of a cliff.

Personal courage could look like taking a class on a new topic, applying for that job that feels like a stretch, or making an off-the-beaten-path investment. Or perhaps your version of courage could be going skydiving, stepping onto a dance floor, or signing up for a 10k run.

Professional courage takes many forms. Like calling out someone's behavior. Or marching up to your boss and proudly declaring you quit. Smaller moments can be just as courageous, like

- Speaking up at the end of a meeting and asking if the group would consider changing the meeting format.
- Letting a peer leader know that how they talk to women comes across as mansplaining.
- Taking an initiative that could put you at risk if it fails, yet believing in your heart that it will succeed.

These less visible moments can take even more courage.

Whether at work or elsewhere, the experience of fear and courage can vary. We can feel a jumbled mess of fear, anxiety, hope, and expectations. We might need someone to pump us up, or we might be able to summon courage all on our own. And what about opportunities for courage we didn't see coming? When we are forced to act in the moment?

I was doing a multi-stage race, an all-day event involving kayaking, running, mountain biking, and rappelling. At one point, I found myself at the base of a 330-foot cliff with ropes hanging down what amounted to a vertical football field. My task was to drop my bike and run six miles uphill to the point where the ropes were anchored to the top of the cliff.

I'm not a heights guy, and a mental snapshot of those dangling ropes is seared into my brain. The view from the bottom was all I could think of the whole run-up to the top. When I arrived, I was tired, and I knew the only way to continue was to gear up and get attached. Each rope had a spotter who checked gear and made sure you were good to go. My spotter looked me over and said I was ready. I backed up to the cliff's edge, rope in hand, and froze.

He looked at me and said, "What's up?"

Wasn't it obvious? I said, "I'm completely freaked out."

Was it courage that got me down via the rope? I want to think so, but the reality is that a stranger got me over the edge. He told me to do exactly what he said and never take my eyes off his eyes. Somehow, he got me over the edge.

People I share my story with say my rappelling down a 330-foot cliff was courageous, but I'm still unsure. The result may have looked courageous, but the process felt like much less. True, the guy didn't push me over. My own tiny step backward got me moving downward. But I certainly don't feel any pride knowing I didn't rationally summon courage from deep within.

When a donor donated $500M to a cancer research program, I found myself at the center of constructing a new building for a research group. The head of the group proudly proclaimed the building would be unlike any other facility. Cancer research in general is a combination of doing science and raising funds. Program heads spend substantial time soliciting dollars, often competing against others in their field. How would this facility be different? Instead of individual researchers chasing their own funding and running their own programs, multiple researchers would work together without the need to constantly raise research funds.

When I first met with the research head and he explained this vision, I asked if he expected the building to create an environment where the researchers would collaborate. He said yes. In front of my boss, I told this important person that the researchers he was talking about weren't nice people. In fact, my team had built research facilities for all of them, and we quickly learned they were all highly difficult to work with. Now he wanted all of them to suddenly join hands and work together? Happiness wasn't going to happen. Unless...

Unless we simultaneously got the building design underway and worked on transforming the researchers into a team. At that moment, my boss inhaled, sucked all the air out of the room, and held his breath. What would the leader say? I just told him his team was full of arrogant brainiacs who didn't know how to work together.

I thought my words were practical. Matter of fact. My boss thought I was being very, very risky. Was I being courageous? I think so.

Back to my kayaking adventure. I had to be courageous for the sake of my kid, who, unlike me, was eagerly looking for alligators. Then we found one.

My son got excited, pointed, and shouted, "THERE'S ONE!" Two eyes above the water, swimming straight toward our boat. And fast! I have no idea how fast the gator was moving, but it felt like a hundred miles an hour like a black torpedo just under the surface of the water. I was already two hours into our paddle, hot, sweaty, and tired. My heart rate soared, and my body felt like I was spiking a fever. All I could think about was how that alligator would T-bone our plastic boat, flip us into the water, and eat us both.

THINK AND DISCUSS (PART THREE)

- When did you have the chance to be courageous but backed away?
- Where do you see an opportunity to be courageous this week?
- When have you watched someone lean into courage? What did you observe?
- Where could you help someone act courageously? What can you do?

Courage takes the form of risk and reward. Do well and you win. But if you do poorly, does that necessarily mean you lost?

Before you speak up in a meeting and challenge the boss, you weigh the outcomes. The risk is looking very bad in front of the person who signs your paycheck. The reward is the possibility that your boss sees you as a star.

My alligator fears came from deep within me and stuck with me every minute we were on the water. Was I courageous the entire time? I want to think so. I certainly didn't overcome my fear of alligators in those three hours. I was just as nervous at the end as I was at the start. I was exhausted from the heat, the paddling, and my constant vigilance. I was never relaxed, though at times I was able to enjoy the moment. My son really liked the time we spent on the water. So did I. For me, the part that felt like genuine courage was letting myself be aware of my fear, which hit me in an instant with zero time to prepare, then managing my attitude and behaviors for the next several hours.

This level of effort felt tremendous, and the situation only involved the two of us. What happens when you're asked to be courageous on behalf of many others?

The Ryan Holiday book Courage is Calling contains three parts: "Fear,"

"Courage," and "The Heroic." The entire third section tells the stories of people who displayed courage for causes much larger than themselves. From Sparta to Vietnam to the Middle East, some saw the need for courage coming, while others found themselves mustering courage at a moment's notice. All the stories describe selfless acts where people chose courage for the greater good—a movement, ending a war, or simply surviving. Each story portrays courage at the highest level.

While you may never have the opportunity to be courageous like the heroes in Holiday's book, courageous moments happen more often than you think. When you see someone nearby who has a chance to be courageous, join in. When you act in a way to support that person, you, too, are indeed courageous.

CHAPTER 15

Sacrifice

LIFE PRESENTS US WITH CHOICES. WHATEVER WE CHOOSE, THE OTHER OPTIONS OFTEN DISAPPEAR. SOMETIMES THEY'RE GONE FOREVER.

When you're a kid, you get to pick a piece of Halloween candy from a neighbor's bowl of goodies. Pick the one you really want. But be careful not to pick the wrong one.

You get what you want. But at what cost?

The other choices will be left behind. You weigh the trade-offs. You considered all the options, and there were two you really liked. You do the quick math on how many of each you already have, how many additional houses you plan to hit, the likelihood of receiving more, and your frequency of consumption of each kind in the past six months.

Okay, that's a stretch for any kid when it comes to candy. The point is this: When faced with options, we consider a multitude of factors before we settle on our choice. And in picking something, we sacrifice something else.

Yes, sacrifice. Why apply such a big word to such an insignificant situation? Because sacrifice by definition results in pain. Does picking the wrong candy result in pain? It could. Maybe your assumptions and expectations are wrong. What if the piece of candy you think is in your bag isn't there? You would feel disappointment, sadness, and pain.

Is all pain bad? Yes! That's why it's called pain!

Pain hurts, whether the distress is physical, mental, or emotional. Though if pain can make you stronger, is it truly bad? If you're training for an athletic event, you will feel pain along the way. Your body will hurt. Yet you tell yourself the pain is worth it. The physical pain you feel is just your body's way of telling you that you're working hard, getting stronger, building up for the moment when you will run the race, ride the ride, or climb the mountain. The pain will help you succeed.

Do you justify discomfort in the same way when you're pressured to give up your non-work hours for work? What if you need to take a super important call during your kid's sporting event? What do you do? Your kid will certainly feel emotional pain if you miss the game, though your reputation at work will suffer pain if you say no. It's a much tougher decision than picking between pieces of candy.

THINK AND DISCUSS (PART ONE)

- What does sacrifice mean to you?
- How do your upbringing, values, beliefs, and experience influence your definition?
- What examples have you experienced of tradeoffs—taking one thing and giving up another? What sacrifices result if you attempt to juggle both?
- How do you feel when you sacrifice?

When we're young, we experience sacrifice primarily as choices between simple wants. Pick this—or that. As we grow up, our sacrifices have significant consequences.

The decisions of adolescence often come with long-term impacts. As children grow through middle and high school, they pick sports, clubs, and activities. There's not enough time to do everything, so they're forced to make choices. If I play soccer, I won't be able to run cross country, since they take place in the same season. Or there's a choice between practicing the same sport year-round or participating in multiple sports and clubs. Choices teach kids that they can't do it all, and for some kids, the pressure to choose wisely begins early.

It's easy to project onto others our understanding of sacrifice. We might force our kids to get up early on Saturdays for practice, because that toughened us up when we were young. Those early practices taught us responsibility. We sacrificed staying out late the night before. Or gave up sleeping in. Our social lives may have suffered, though the sacrifice was worth it. Hard work and training may have been painful. Suffering followed by victory confirms that sacrificing comfort leads to success.

And with the blink of an eye, we're done choosing between school activities and out in the working world, where sacrifice takes on a whole new meaning.

Sacrifices at work are usually nuanced. Fuzzy. We often must think through potential outcomes. Like that time you were asked to stay late or work a weekend. What did you feel in that instant? Your internal dialogue most likely went something like *Should I work this weekend? I can't say no, can I? Should I? But there's that promotion I want, and working this weekend would move me closer to getting a raise. No one told me, but that's how things seem to work around here.* Or perhaps your experiences at work are more direct. Like the quiet conversations at work about how people start families and get passed over for promotions. Or positions might require the sacrifice of personal time in the form of being on call or traveling.

Sacrifice at work causes a variety of pain—strain on families, emotional exhaustion, and having zero work–life balance. These sound extreme, and in fact, they are. But that doesn't mean they're uncommon. Adding to the complexity is that sacrifices at work often start small and grow slowly over time, maybe without you even realizing it.

Take Stan, a retail manager. When he first took over a store, he knew the job came with more responsibilities. Regular visits from his district manager were new, and he felt he needed to make a good impression. Stan regularly worked long hours. He kept telling his family the situation was temporary, that once he made a strong impression on his new boss, he could return to normal working hours. Over a few months, more responsibilities piled on. Fewer resources were available for bookkeeping and finance, so Stan took on even more hours helping with the numbers. Then, margins thinned, labor had to be reduced. Again, Stan felt pressured to step up and give more time to the store.

As the months went on, the hope that these "temporary" situations would end slipped away. Stan had less time for self-care. Less time for family.

While he convinced himself he was doing everything to advance his professional career, he was sacrificing his family, friends, and health. While his wife encouraged him to speak up about the situation, Stan felt the culture of the company didn't create an environment that allowed him to safely speak his mind.

Stan's situation certainly isn't unique. For many managers and mid-level leaders, implied and inferred expectations abound. When left unchecked, these workplace sacrifices lead to even more than what Stan experienced, such as reduced creativity, energy, and burnout.

What happens when we consciously choose sacrifice? When we deliberately forego the promotion because we know that the added pay comes with added responsibilities? For years, I watched senior-level people work countless hours. While preaching self-care and providing wellness programs, these leaders suffered from weight gain, chronic disease, and constant stress. These leaders would say they were sacrificing themselves for the greater good, the next job, or whatever reasons they convinced themselves of.

Were their sacrifices intentional trade-offs? Or were they unthinkingly absorbed from the environment and culture? And what about those who are led? What did they see? That to get the next job, the next promotion, will require the same sacrifices?

THINK AND DISCUSS (PART TWO)

- What types of sacrifice have you experienced—physical, relationships, kids, or something else?
- Where have your sacrifices in decision-making caused you to suffer?
- What types of pains have you experienced because of your sacrifices—physical, mental, emotional, or other?
- What sacrifices at work have you experienced?

Have you ever had to choose between paying rent or buying food? Life gets truly gut-wrenching when you're forced to choose between needs— rent, food, electricity, clothes, and more.

Sometimes the pain of the sacrifice turns acute. Or even life-and-death serious. Consider four types of sacrifice:

- Sacrifice of wants: You put off buying a car because you're saving to buy a house.
- Sacrifice of values: You feel pressure not to follow your values.
- Sacrifice of needs: You're forced to pick between human necessities, like food and shelter.
- Sacrifice of time: You must choose where to spend your time.

Being forced to choose between two wants can be considered a luxury by some. Picking between two purchases, two weekend outings, or two vacation destinations is a dilemma many humans only dream of facing. The sacrifice seems to have a very limited impact, and the pain caused by losing out on one alternative is minimal at most.

The game steps up when your value system is challenged. Consider Stan, our retail manager. He certainly valued spending time with friends and family, and his work slowly eroded the strength of that value within Stan. We could ask why he recognized it too late, or question why he didn't stop the madness sooner. For most people, Stan's situation doesn't happen overnight. It's a slow burn, a frog in the pan scenario. You don't realize what is happening until it has happened.

One resource limited for all of us is time. Claiming we know its value isn't the same as spending our time with intention. Does treasuring time mean we're supposed to be efficient, effective, and functional at all hours? We must ask ourselves what those three terms mean. We must choose where we spend our time creating, resting, functioning, and working. There still exists a mindset that "busy" is a laudable way to describe ourselves. Are we busy doing the right things? We say we're so busy we don't have time to read, yet we have time to scroll on social media.

Take the self-evaluation a step further and ask what we're scrolling through and why. Do we allow ourselves a few minutes to scroll, laugh at a few jokes, like our family's pictures, stay updated on old friends, then stop? Or do we consciously recognize we're tired or overwhelmed and need to focus on something mindless for a while? Scrolling isn't so bad. But are we effectively regenerating, or are we missing out on more important things?

THINK AND DISCUSS (PART THREE)

- How does our attitude toward sacrifice impact our own choices and how we judge others' choices?
- When has a choice felt like a sacrifice in the moment that later turned out to have a valuable outcome?
- What are we teaching others about sacrifice through our actions, words, thoughts, work, and behaviors?
- Where can we be intentional with our approach to sacrifice?

For many years, I was extremely cautious about expending extra time at work. Some might call it selfish. I was intentional about limiting what I worked on above and beyond my core job duties.

Why did I choose this approach? Wasn't I jeopardizing a promotion?

It took me a while to gain a longer-term view of life. I still wasn't sure of my purpose. But I realized I wasn't in a forever job. It wasn't a role I could ride to retirement. Once I achieved a bit of clarity, I was free of all the implied and inferred expectations that my environment and I placed on me. I made the conscious decision to choose where to spend my time. To the best of my ability, I limited the "other duties as assigned," optional meetings, and awkward social gatherings. I could focus on my core job, and not surprisingly, I found myself with time.

When I shared this approach with a few executives, it was met with surprise and argument. I was told I was lucky. They could never get away with that. There was so much heaped on their plate that the mere thought of saying no to anything was beyond realistic.

Consider what these executives and I sacrificed in our diametrically different approaches.

My approach had an interesting impact on my team. In our one-to-ones, I found myself asking where they spent their time. The answers varied, and with some digging, I found most people allowed others to dictate where they spent their time. We had already created a culture that urged aligning the right work with the right people, and honest reflections by team members were safe. No one had a problem filling their time, meaning many realized they were allowed to pause and ponder where they wanted to spend time, where they brought value, and where they could step back or step out. We openly spoke about how sacrificing attendance and participation in these areas could impact them professionally and personally.

When you feel free to do an honest cost/benefit analysis and make your choices accordingly, these are the kinds of questions you ask yourself:

- Should I sacrifice my family time for this work project?
- Should I trade comfort for pain while training for a race?
- Should I risk my health just this once and eat fast food?
- Should I wreck my team's health and job satisfaction to meet an unrealistic deadline?

I like those questions.

When we realize what we're sacrificing and make intentional decisions, it's easier to choose to live according to our highest values. How we decide what to sacrifice is just as important as what we sacrifice. Consider your values and what you hold most dear. Ponder what outside influences are impacting your decision on what to sacrifice and why. Do they have a right to tell you what to sacrifice—or not? Most don't—but some do!

If people in your workplace wonder what the expectations are (and I guarantee many do, including you), start this conversation on sacrifice. What are they giving up? Why? How? The drivers behind those decisions will begin a process that will strengthen your connections and improve the lives of everyone around you—including your own.

CHAPTER 16

Communication

IT'S NOT JUST WHAT YOU SAY, IT'S HOW YOU SAY IT.

"She just doesn't listen to me." "I don't think people are hearing me even though they say they are." "No matter what I try, people say I need to improve my communication." "The secret to success is communication— just communicate!"

Communication is inescapably essential to every aspect of our lives. That doesn't make it easy!

Some people naturally expose the contents of their mind and heart to the world without filters. Others withhold communication and only share with intentionality. CliftonStrengths describes the Communication strength like this: "People exceptionally talented in the Communication theme generally find it easy to put their thoughts into words. They are good conversationalists and presenters." The definition adds that those strong with Communication possess the ability to have their "word pictures pique their interest, sharpen their world, and inspire them to act."

Should we all adapt our communication to fit that definition? Take naturally deep thinkers, who withhold their thoughts until they capture enough information to fully form a coherent thought. They sit through meetings in complete silence until they have something profound to say. Do they need to work on their communication?

THINK AND DISCUSS (PART ONE)

- When does communication come easily for you? What words describe what that feels like?
- When do you struggle to communicate?
- To what types of people or in what environments do you communicate easily?
- What people never quite get what you're trying to say?

What is communication? Is it: a) the exchange of information, ideas, and feelings; b) a social contact; c) written correspondence; d) all of the above; or e) none of the above?

Based on these definitions, we could theoretically improve our communication simply by increasing its quantity. Talk more. Write more. Express more. Is more communication the answer?

Probably not. Middle managers, for example, can easily create communication mishaps every time they open their mouths. Wanting to be likable and gain the trust of their direct reports, they overshare. Maybe they criticize their company to build rapport or get laughs by making snide comments about leaders. On the surface, this can feel authentic or transparent, but is it truly useful? If it strengthens one set of relationships at the expense of others, is this communication effective?

Middle managers also field communications from up, down, and across the organization. Take Vanessa, a leader with more than a dozen people constantly supplying her with information, thousands of emails, voicemails, and messages every year, which she is supposed to consider and synthesize. The flood of communication became so overwhelming that she simply quit paying attention. If she had a problem or a question, she just reached out to whoever knew the answer. Talk about a time saver! No longer was she bound by the daily ritual of reading and processing information.

How was this style of communication received by others? She received frequent reactions of "I already sent that to you," "You asked for this three times already," and "That's in the report I sent you Monday." At first, people tried to be helpful and give her the benefit of the doubt, believing her busyness caused their miscommunications. Sympathy morphed into resentment. Vanessa was a leader with substantial power. No one felt they could say out loud that her approach was frustrating and time-consuming for those who worked with her.

Why couldn't they speak the truth to Vanessa? It didn't fall within the communication norms of their company. While trust and transparency were touted as important in the workplace, the reality was that employees were routinely passive in how they responded to aggressive communicators like Vanessa.

Communications experts describe four communication styles:

1.   Passive Communication

Passive communicators rarely speak up for themselves. They feel more comfortable addressing others' wants and needs. They avoid confrontation and can appear submissive. This tendency becomes clear when someone says something hurtful or harmful, and the passive communicator doesn't speak up. They reason that the other person has more power, or they don't want to upset anyone. One challenge for the passive communicator is that all the things they wish they could say build up inside over time, and without a means of release, they come out in unproductive ways. Consider a neighbor who bothers you regularly with their actions, but you never say anything. You figure it's too much trouble. You convince yourself you should just let it go, yet the feelings fester inside you.

2.   Aggressive Communication

Aggressive communicators are so confident in their positions that they often fail to listen to others' thoughts and opinions. They can be pushy, talk down to people, or bluntly declare, "You're wrong!" Unsurprisingly, this style creates tension. Aggressive communicators get angry at others, express what they're thinking, then excuse themselves as being authentic, transparent, or passionate.

There's no question that aggressive communicators create negative experiences. But is the aggressive style ever warranted? People in safety roles argue that it is. They know best what's safe and right, and they often deploy an aggressive style to keep people from harm.

3. Passive-aggressive Communication

Passive-aggressive communicators struggle to speak their point directly. Their words, intentions, and behaviors aren't aligned. They may verbally support an idea, but their tone, body language, and facial expressions disagree. Recipients of their communication feel confused and pressured to figure out what the person truly means. While most of us dislike passive-aggressive communication, we often tolerate it in situations where confrontation is discouraged or speaking honestly could cause harm. For example, when an extremist uncle spouts off at your next family gathering, should you speak up—or do you overlook the behavior as long as it doesn't cause too much harm in the moment?

4. Assertive Communication

Assertive communicators express their opinions, thoughts, and ideas in a way that shows confidence. They advocate for what they want, whether personal gain or speaking up for others. Their words match their behaviors and expressions.

We prefer to see ourselves as kind, enlightened, and mature, and we therefore think we always communicate assertively. We know what we want, advocate for it, represent others who can't or don't speak for themselves, and we always communicate clearly and effectively.

As a mentor who always had an eloquent way with words would say— really?

Consider these examples:
- A neighbor allows their dog to run wild throughout the neighborhood, including charging kids on bikes and barking aggressively. The neighbor just laughs it off, yelling at his dog while saying "sorry!" How do you say to your neighbor that their dog is obnoxious and potentially dangerous?
- At the grocery store, someone parks their cart in the middle of the aisle while browsing for an item, making it impossible for you to pass. Do you say something—or maneuver slowly until they notice—or even bump your cart into theirs—and then apologize and say, "Oh, no problem. It's ok."
- At work, as you exchange information in the same old weekly or monthly meeting, are you consistently assertive, or do you

occasionally check out?
- When the fire alarm goes off, do you take charge, give directions, or get yourself out? How do you communicate your choice?
- When you're with family or friends deciding where to go out for dinner, are you open to suggestions—or do you stand by and let others decide—or do you push what you want on others because you're sure they'll love your choice?
- When you're in a leadership role, what factors influence your communication style? If a deadline is fast approaching, does your approach change—as opposed to trudging along in the normal course of business?

Stress, urgency, and apparent risk or danger clearly influence how we communicate. The situation, environment, and context all play a part in how we proceed. In those moments, do we let the demands of the moment direct how we communicate—or do we pause long enough to consciously choose the best approach?

THINK AND DISCUSS (PART TWO)

- What is your natural communication style?
- Think of examples where you expressed yourself using each of the four communication styles. How did your style impact outcomes?
- What communication practices, guidelines, or rules do you follow?
- What recent situations have caused you to communicate differently than your natural style?

Communication has two parts: the information being conveyed, and the listening, understanding, and absorption of that information.

We can convey meaning through spoken words, actions, and writing. We can listen with our ears, eyes, and minds. For an accurate exchange of information, both parts of the communication process must be present. Transmitting a message without someone receiving it isn't communication. Neither are our one-way efforts of talking louder, repeating ourselves, or saying the same thing with similar words.

Technology increases the quantity of our communication without necessarily increasing its quality. Email, virtual meetings, social media, and text messages are technically communication since they exchange information and ideas, but how effective are they? How many emails have you read where you thought the sender was a jerk? How many emails have you sent that required you to explain yourself because the recipient thought you were stupid or insensitive? How many emails have you read that you completely forgot?

I'm not sure the bare words of a social media post can be considered communication. Remember that communication has two sides, involving sharing and receiving information or an idea. The receiving portion of communication developed its own body of knowledge into the art of listening. "Active," "critical," "empathetic," "effective," "reflective," "deep," "workplace," "passive" are just a few types of listening highlighted by researchers to help us understand how we can listen better.

Some individuals listen intently and with empathy all the time, but those people are rare. Most of us have so much to do and so much on our minds that when people share things that don't seem to directly impact our world, we only half-listen—our sort-of and kind-of paying attention, nodding, and "uh-huh" behaviors. The moment we conclude that the person attempting to communicate with us isn't saying much that matters to us personally, we put on a nice face and appear to listen, but in reality, we hear just enough to make the other person feel we're listening even though we're not.

People with high emotional intelligence can easily read when others tune them out. It doesn't matter which communication style senders employ. They all can get the same half-hearted attention, and as a society, we generally tolerate this behavior. We don't expect more than surface communication when the barista asks how our day is going. The acceptable answer is short and brief. We don't use the question as an opportunity to share intimate details about our terrible day, from running out of milk to the cat throwing up to needing to find time for an oil change. We share the social belief that being brief is the proper etiquette.

The same goes for work. We focus on quick exchanges of information and usually avoid complex topics such as religion, politics, and personal and family health. Are we communicating? Yes. But not deeply. We stick to topics we mutually understand to be safe. And we squirm and search for an exit when anyone veers from the norms.

Communication of surface-level—that is, safe—topics feels easiest in our transaction-based world. I have a question, tell me the answer, thank you, communication complete. Perhaps we have a friend at work who we share personal conversations with. Or our company tries various ways to help people connect—happy hours, company picnics, sharing pet pictures, and days dedicated to Hawaiian shirts or sports jerseys. Do these efforts help us communicate with each other? Perhaps if we give them a try. They may provide openings to strengthen relationships and build trust to share ideas and values, which can allow us to lean into deeper and more complex communication.

Have you considered how you expect others to communicate with you?

Matt wrote a "How to work with Matt" guide for his team members at work. He shared who he is, how he sees the world, and how he communicates. One of the more important areas of this guide is where Matt discusses how to communicate with him. He makes this clear point: "No matter what, don't dance around an issue or try to lead me somewhere. If it's on your mind, just say it." This sounds good, and Matt is cognizant that his position as a leader often makes people feel like they need this explicit permission. He continues, "When you tell me something, I will ask questions and go silent from time to time as I think and process what you're sharing. I'm not judging you, nor am I upset. I want you to know that our business is important and that we need to share information without fear of each other. I know my silence can feel unsettling in the moment, and rest assured—I'm still listening and appreciate when you are forthright."

Matt sets a clear expectation that he wants to be told all important information—good and bad—and won't take it out on the messenger. Further, he states how people can expect him to react— silence, thinking, questions—and he wants people to understand what he's doing. The person engaging him in conversation shouldn't wonder if he's still listening. And he doesn't want them to make up their own interpretation of what's happening.

This is Matt's best attempt to send a message clearly, intervening before people try to guess if he's mad, upset, or ready to explode. It's his way of releasing them from fear. He's clear about how people who work with him can expect their communication to feel.

THINK AND DISCUSS (PART THREE)

- In what areas or instances can you improve your communication?
- When and how should your approach to communication change based on the situation?
- Where can you help someone improve their communication with others (people other than you)?
- What opportunities can you see for you to work with others to improve communication?

How do we know we are communicating effectively?

When what we say is being heard? When we ourselves listen with intent and purpose, allowing other people to feel heard?

First, we must discern if we are communicating with intention, starting with choosing the right style for the situation. Then we must seek genuine feedback from people we trust and count on them to be honest. Finally, we must listen to their feedback with an open mind, recognize when we get defensive when receiving feedback, and practice our listening skills.

How we communicate is one of our most human-centric skills. Practicing, seeking feedback, and actively looking for ways to improve our ability to communicate is one of the most powerful ways we can become better people.

CHAPTER 17

Self-Discipline and Self-Control

MAKE YOUR BED. DO YOUR CHORES. GET GOOD GRADES. GET A JOB, GO TO WORK ON TIME, AND GRIND AWAY.

If I say "discipline," your mind might jump to your own habits and routines. Or you might recall key points you absorbed from people who tried to teach or train you. Or you might think of how discipline was imposed on you by others.

Depending on when and where you grew up, you experienced a high or low level of expectations—or something in between. At home, discipline comes in a wide range of actions and reactions. Some parents are stricter than others—as in your homework must be done before you hang out with friends. Other parents allow you to play first—as long as your homework is done by bedtime or whenever it's due.

As a kid, school was your full-time job. Discipline there might have felt punitive. While getting your backside paddled may have given way to detention and other non-physical punishments, students now find motivational carrots are more common than sticks.

How did you experience discipline at home? At school? In your neighborhood? On teams? In early jobs? Did adults state their expectations clearly? Or did you need to guess?

I grew up with chores. Plenty of them. With six people sharing a modest space, we had little choice but to each do our part to keep the house functioning properly. I took out the trash, my brother swept, and my sisters did the dishes. Daily. Without any one of these disciplines, our house would have quickly descended into messy chaos. Saturday was designated for bigger chores like bathrooms, laundry, mopping, vacuuming, and more. Our parents regulated and enforced these routines, and even when weekend activities disrupted our schedules, we still had to finish our chores.

When I moved out at age 18, it was no surprise that I rebelled against these expectations. I quit cleaning. Mostly. I skipped church. Often. I decided my new freedom relieved me of parental rules. While I enjoyed loosening their grip, it wasn't long before my apartment was a FEMA-level disaster.

Curiously, my inbuilt discipline kept me exercising and eating healthily. Self-discipline compelled me to brush my teeth, which had a dynamic of risk and reward. I wasn't sure if I had brushed because I had learned I would get in trouble if I didn't. Or maybe it was anticipated consequences—bad breath in the short term or teeth falling out some distant day.

It makes me wonder about our adult self-discipline. Where does it come from? Is it fear? Or risk versus reward? Or a desire to do right? Or something else?

It helps to clarify terms. "Discipline" is something others do to us. "Self-discipline" and "self-control" are things we do for ourselves to regulate our emotions and behaviors.

Self-discipline is saying "yes" to a positive thing, and self-control is saying "no" to something negative. Self-discipline helps us lean into habits and continue to do what we believe to be good. Self-control prevents us from doing bad or harmful things. It empowers us to refuse the donut, keep from aligning with bad people, or refrain from spending money on things we don't need.

THINK AND DISCUSS (PART ONE)

- How did you experience discipline growing up?
- What are your definitions of self-discipline and self-control?

- Which dynamic felt more important at home and school: saying no to bad things or saying yes to good?
- As an adult, in what areas do you exert self-discipline? How about self-control?

> ### *Every human being struggles with some aspect of self-discipline or self-control—or both.*

Most of us wish we had the willpower to be more self-disciplined. To eat better. Exercise regularly. Sleep more. Stop scrolling. Invest our discretionary hours in something other than technology. We envy the people who form and follow good habits, yet we might justify our own behaviors with equal energy. Who has time to make the bed every morning? Why bother when it only gets messed up again in the evening?

As for self-control, most people claim to value things like refraining from overeating or giving vent to road rage. Fidgety kids are told to sit still and control themselves. But how far does our self-control go? Blurting out in a meeting, telling teammates our company sucks, or trash-talking others behind their backs— are these examples of being authentic or examples of poor self-control?

How we decide whether behavior is acceptable gets even more puzzling. When people violate a social norm, dress however they want, or speak without filters, are they displaying a lack of self-control or being authentic? As with all complex matters, the answer is, "It depends!" Having a high degree of situational awareness and intentionally choosing how we behave in a specific moment is one key to answering the question. Thinking before acting is another. Although we can't see the motives of others, we can look inside ourselves and be honest about our own self-control or lack of it.

Self-control can be positive when it prevents us from putting ourselves in harm's way. It can keep us from doing or saying the wrong thing at the wrong time. And self-control is undergirded by the good habits we acquire through self-discipline. By putting in the work and practicing how we want to act when the pressure is on, we find it easier to fall back on those good patterns we have developed over time. When we have little to no discipline to call on, our self-control may vanish.

Picture a sports team. Your coach and teammates can only carry you so far. You have to want to get better. You must put in the work—giving your all at practice, drilling at home, and catching quick moments to practice. Self-discipline ensures you get good rest, eat well, and study the game on your own. Sure, it's easier to stay up late, eat poorly, or let your focus drift at practice, but you'll pay for it on game day. Your good habits and hard work before the game directly impact your performance. Without diligent preparation, your performance is a gamble.

The same goes for any aspect of our lives.

The direct connection between sleeping well and physical activity is obvious, yet are you aware that something as simple as making the bed each morning can drive your performance? Make Your Bed by Admiral William H. McRaven conveys the necessity of starting each day by accomplishing one thing. Making your bed develops a habit of achieving something small yet important every day, and accumulated small acts are monumental in building good habits and developing patterns of self-discipline. Only by putting in the effort to do small things can you achieve big things.

We might want the money, fame, and accolades enjoyed by successful people without recognizing the years of work and effort that made those things possible. And not just the major habits directly responsible for success, but the minute-by-minute self-discipline and self-control that paved the way. Success is a result, a byproduct, of doing the work.

There are countless stories of successful people who labored hard to succeed in their chosen field. Kobe Bryant was always the first of his teammates to practice. Coach Pete Carroll of the Seattle Seahawks was not only the first to arrive each day but the last to leave. (His long hours were so obvious that the team's star running back, Marshawn Lynch, once asked Pete if he ever slept.) Musicians clock long hours in the studio. Business leaders pour their lives into the business. But hours at work aren't the whole story. When pressed, these people always cite the importance of self-discipline and self-control in other areas of their lives, including relationships, mental health, off-seasons, relaxation and recovery, and, for some, making their bed each day.

THINK AND DISCUSS (PART TWO)

- Where do people need more self-discipline?
- In what areas do you wish you had better self-discipline and self-control?

- What expectations of self-control do you have of others—family, friends, colleagues, and strangers?
- When do you exert too much self-control on yourself? On others?

When people around us don't match our level of self-discipline and self-control, we judge them.

The driver who fails to let others merge. The coworker who's always gone on smoke breaks. The manager who doesn't hold employees accountable. We observe, and we judge.

Our perceptions cut the other way as well. When others have different levels of self-discipline and self-control than we do, we might admire them. Or we might justify our own choices while criticizing them as uptight or unreal.

As humans, judgment is one of our strongest natural inclinations.

Our upbringing, school, work, and assorted life experiences all come together to form our patterns of self-discipline and self-control. Our core beliefs translate into critical thoughts. If we were raised to brush our teeth twice a day, then we're more likely to put the same expectations on others. Same with our patterns of eating, exercising, and clocking in and out of work. Those of us who empty our email inboxes every day believe others should do the same.

If we pause and examine what we expect of ourselves, it's easy to see how often we project our expectations on others. But are our choices regarding self-discipline and self-control appropriate for everyone? For our kids? For coworkers? For strangers we know nothing about?

Maybe. Or maybe not!

Before we hold others accountable for our own internal convictions, we must truly grapple with our belief systems. If we have too little self-discipline and self-control, others who follow our lead may inadvertently bring harm on themselves.

What about too much self-discipline and self-control? Is there such a thing? How does that play out?

A wife asked her husband, "Can you try to be more passionate?" Her husband answered, "I've developed too much self-discipline and self-control to be passionate!" Through countless experiences, the husband had come to believe that controlling emotions was an expectation without exception, acting emotionally was unprofessional, and overly emotional people don't get ahead at work.

This approach can indeed be a sign of self-control, but is our societal beatdown of emotions at work healthy? Warranted? Or does it inhibit relationships, innovation, and happiness?

Consider a typical day. In meeting after meeting, we tolerate a few minutes of small talk, get down to business, end in a hurry, and rush to the next meeting. Along the way, we may sneak in a few minutes for lunch, perhaps with colleagues, where we chat about the game, kids, or news. Then back to work. Finally, after work, we vent to our friends and family. Or we just collapse into bed, ground down by a long day that allowed us to be human for only a few scattered moments. For all the rest of our hours, we were expected to be productive. And emotions don't equate to productivity.

Some people put things like analysis, efficiency, and high output at the top of their priority list. Connections and relationships happen after work. Self-discipline and self-control rule the day, and the results speak for themselves. Or do they? Perhaps the results remain elusive. Or the highest and best results never show up.

I think there's a reason why. Performance is about more than our personal habits. It's about people working together, and the best work happens when people bond. Maybe not as best friends, but with the basic connections and relationships people crave. When self-discipline and self-control rule our days, we lose the ability to be human. And often that means results fall short.

THINK AND DISCUSS (PART THREE)

- Where can you improve your self-discipline and self-control?
- Where should you give yourself more flexibility and lighten up?
- How can you determine with others what healthy self-discipline and self-control look like—and where too much gets in the way of higher goals?
- How can you help others develop healthy self-discipline and self-control?

We've all met people who are uptight, and others who are free-flowing, taking each moment as it comes. Some of us plan, and some wing it. Some run their lives with extreme discipline, and others take each day and hour as it comes. And we believe that our way is the right way. When we make our bed—or don't—we congratulate ourselves. When others go against our own way of doing life, we judge.

How can we find our way through this crucial issue?

First, start by understanding your own beliefs and behaviors toward self-discipline and self-control. Why do you do what you do?

Next, start a conversation with others. Is your level of self-discipline and self-control allowing you to live your best life? Is it too much, too little, or just right? Study and reflect on all the parts of your day, like work, home, exercise, eating, relaxation, hobbies, and relationships. Determine these things with others rather than by yourself. Why? You'll only interpret and justify your own behaviors through your own pre-established way of looking at the world. You'll only make minor tweaks. And you also need external affirmation. It's important to hear where people who care about you think you get it right.

Finally, reflect on how you project your expectations of yourself onto others. Look at when and where you do this. Again, talk to a trusted ally about what you uncover. Discuss if you're seeing each situation for the truth. A friend, spouse, or colleague will help you.

Self-discipline and self-control are vital to our lives. When we exert them with intention, each is a powerful force that allows us to live well.

Your own journey of self-discovery might be complemented by walking with someone else through theirs. Going through this process along with another human is highly beneficial.

One final thought to ponder. How do self-discipline and self-control change throughout life? The levels appropriate in your teens won't be the same in your thirties, fifties, or seventies. While decades of age are a useful measure, life events such as getting married, having kids, career changes, and household moves impact what you need from each. In these pivotal moments, reflect and be intentional about your own expectations, and share those expectations with someone close to you.

CHAPTER 18

———

Time

HOW DO YOU SPEND YOUR TIME? HOW ACCURATELY DO YOU KNOW? EVEN MORE IMPORTANTLY, WHY DO YOU SPEND YOUR TIME AS YOU DO? WHAT DRIVES YOUR YEARS, MONTHS, DAYS, AND HOURS.

I wasn't looking for an in-flight conversation when the stranger seated next to me started in. He asked about my work and where I was going. When I asked the same about him, he unfurled his entire life story. Or at least enough to give me the impression he was trying to convince himself of something. For twenty-plus years, this guy worked to build an import company, hunting for American companies that wanted things made, then brokering deals with Chinese manufacturers. He was constantly flying back and forth across the Pacific, and he traveled extensively across China to source goods, troubleshoot, and manage the logistics and red tape of high-volume imports.

This work so consumed my seatmate that he lost all his relationships—wife, kids, extended family, and friends. He toiled to build an empire, and now he was chatting me up. Having made his fortune and left the business, he spent his days doing two things: 1) worrying about losing his money, and 2) trying to reconnect with the people he had lost over the years.

We're often coached to analyze how we spend our time, typically from the viewpoint of how productive we are. Do we consider the forces and values that influence our choices? Plenty of resources can show us how to be more productive. Those might not get at the real issues. Like how well is the guy on the plane currently managing his time? From the perspective of most time management methodologies, he got way more stuff done in his old life. Nowadays, he's not really producing anything, so by that definition, he's wasting daylight. Nevertheless, his current priority of building relationships could be the most important work of his life. I couldn't help but wish him the very best.

Granted, chatty airplane guy is free from many pressures that most other people endure. People still engaged in the workforce know it's imperative to manage time wisely. It requires significant effort, and we take pride in being efficient and effective.

Me? I'm pretty uptight about maximizing my time. For instance, I always make a list before heading to the grocery store. It helps me avoid impulse purchases and wasting time wandering the store and doubling back for missed items. It's efficient, but others might not find my process altogether enjoyable. My wife and I were away for a weekend, and we stopped at a grocery store. As I started to map out meals and our path through the store, she became slightly annoyed. We were standing in front of a bountiful selection of salad fixings when she said, "Can't we just be here and enjoy choosing salad dressing?"

My wife's question profoundly impacted my view of time. I had always treated time as a very limited resource I didn't want to squander. Get stuff done. Hike a trail. Run five miles. Do a work task, then move on to the next. Always be as efficient and productive as possible. I seemed hardwired to see the world as a series of items to check off my list with maximum efficiency. If my activities moved me into a flow where I lost track of time because I was super engaged in what I was doing, that was okay, because even in that freeform state, I was accomplishing things. Check, check, check.

On further reflection of my attitude toward time, I also realized that nearly every moment of my work time was directed by others. I had learned from many mentors and colleagues to never say no to special requests. I always said, "Yes—I'll take on that project." "I'll look into that." "I'll lead the charge." Does someone want me to do something above and beyond my job duties? "Sure, no problem! I can handle it!" I expected that my enthusiasm for tackling everyone's to-dos would get me noticed and promoted. It also had the unintended consequence of rarely having the opportunity to work on what I wanted.

THINK AND DISCUSS (PART ONE)

- Where do you spend your time?
- Do you choose how you spend your time—or is how you spend your time decided for you?
- In what areas do you have control over your time?
- Where do you lack control over your time? Where might you regain control?

Most people aren't in chatty airplane guy's position. They work for a living and will keep at it until they die or retire.

What would you discover if you tracked where you spend your time? Documenting your days can be eye-opening—so try it! For two or three weeks, write down everything you do and how much time you spend on each activity. Then do the math. Sleep will rank high, but so will so many other things. Now pause and evaluate. Are you maximizing your time? Would the time management gods be happy with you?

Bigger question. Must the time gurus be happy with your choices? Objectively, time can be viewed as an opportunity to get things done. But looking at it subjectively changes the conversation. As you check off your boxes and perform at peak efficiency, are you using your time for what matters most to you? How much time do you allot to fulfilling your sense of being—your purpose?

When I was growing up, I watched my older brother get involved in automotive repair. He worked on his own cars, got a job at a shop while in high school, and eventually went to college for aircraft mechanics. Not once in those years did he ever question if mechanics was the right career for him. My father was similar. He always knew he wanted to be involved in electronics, television, and radio. The only question was how. I was midway through college when I mentioned to my father that I was unsure where I was headed. I knew I needed to switch majors, but wasn't sure what new major to select. "I don't understand," he said. "I always knew what I wanted to do, and so did your brother. You seem to have no idea. I just don't get it."

Success stories abound of people who knew early what their talents were and what they wanted to do with their lives. John Belushi was always involved in entertainment, including acting and making people laugh throughout his high school years. He was clear about his intention to become a star and worked hard at his craft. His Blues Brothers partner, Dan Ackroyd, had similar ambitions. He landed in school plays from an early age and intentionally developed his talents. Both found tremendous success.

I've always envied people who knew what they wanted to do with their lives at an early age. Honestly, I admire people who have that clarity at any stage of life. Many of us seem to bounce around, trying this and that, seeking a path that allows us to feel fulfilled.

When you're unsure what you want to do with your life or uncertain if you're living your purpose, time becomes a big question mark. Some fill their time targeting check boxes. They tell themselves they will feel fulfilled when they get a lot done, when they get involved in many things, and when they're asked to take on more responsibilities at work.

What we spend our time on may produce gains in life—money, power, fame, and/or promotion—but we still need to consider some difficult questions. Am I spending my time well? Am I doing what I am supposed to be doing? How do I know? What does my living with purpose feel like? What does my living with intent look like to others?

Besides considering if we're spending our time doing what we should do and living life to the fullest, we must consider the extent to which we can control how we spend our time. At work, am I able to say no? At home? In your community? To myself?

I've found that my daily lists of work and personal items to get done change over time. As my kids entered middle and high school, their activities and events took up a lot of time. During those years, I was asked to sit on the Board of a volunteer group. The opportunity checked a lot of boxes, including career visibility, helping others, and strengthening the community. There were plenty of reasons in the plus column for saying yes. Yet the Board role would put attending my kids' events at risk. After seriously considering the offer, I said no. Right opportunity at the wrong time. My priority for how I spend my time in this season of my life is with my kids. My parents instilled that in me as I was growing up through their own actions, and now that value system came out in full force. I had to choose to say no, and many folks were disappointed.

THINK AND DISCUSS (PART TWO)

- Are you allowed to consider your own needs regarding how you spend your time? Why or why not?
- How intentional are you about how you spend your time?
- Do you think you're spending your time well? How do you know?
- Is it possible to choose what you do with your time without being or feeling selfish? Explain.

> ### *Allowing other people and outside forces to determine how we best use our time can lead to disaster.*

For as long as she could remember, Jamie took on everything. Her work productivity was at its highest ever. She maximized her personal time for sleep, nutrition, exercise, and scheduled relaxation. She even chose an apartment because its kitchen was designed to minimize steps. Eating the same breakfast and lunch every day eliminated wasting time making mundane decisions. Jamie embodied efficiency, and her coworkers and leaders loved her ability to get things done.

Then one day, Jamie's hyperfocus on efficiency and effectiveness suddenly came to a halt. She was unable to gag down the same breakfast she had eaten so many times before. At work, she stared blankly at her screen. As emails piled up, she couldn't find the strength to answer any of them. Meetings came and went, and she had no interest in joining them. She seemed to have lost her drive to do anything.

Except for one email that arrived mid-morning. It came unexpectedly from an old colleague, Jay, who asked Jamie to give him a call. Not knowing the reason for the request set off all her well-trained time management alarms, but for some unknown reason, she called anyway. Jamie was so accustomed to efficient, transactional phone calls that the start of a different kind of conversation felt a bit awkward, yet she quickly found herself happy to catch up and talking about incredibly random things. Jamie surprised herself by asking Jay if he had lunch plans that day. They met and spent the entire afternoon talking.

Back home, Jamie felt strangely elated that she had done absolutely nothing on her to-do list that day. Her entire routine had collapsed. What surprised her was how the day allowed her to see what was truly happening.

Her health had been slowly deteriorating. Her doctors had been telling her to slow down, to give her body and mind time to process life's ups, stresses, and tensions, but Jamie's efficient and effective way of life didn't allow for that. She was checking the boxes, following the regimens, getting the right amount of sleep, eating healthily, and vacationing as appropriate per her schedule, yet she suddenly saw how she was failing her body, mind, and spirit.

In addition, Jamie noticed how her attitude toward work had shifted. Everything on her calendar for the next day felt meaningless. The projects were still on her plate, there were emails to respond to, meetings to attend, and decisions to be made, yet she felt no connection to them. None whatsoever.

And in a moment of clarity, Jamie realized that every bit of the work she did each day was given to her. Piled on her. Sure, she nodded yes and accepted each task. Yet she couldn't remember the last time she made a conscious, proactive decision on how to spend her time.

The next day, Jamie contacted Jay to continue the conversation. She was in awe of his ability to exist with no set schedule, to devote time where it was needed, and to pick and choose what he did each day. How could this be? Jay told Jamie he used to view life just as Jamie did. Until he realized something was missing. A team member came to him, in tears, sharing a highly traumatic personal event. The team member really needed someone to talk to—and she needed someone right then. Jay franticly scanned his calendar, saw emails piling up, mentally calculated what he needed to get done by the end of the day, and when another human being needed his help, he discovered he was weighing giving time to that person versus attending meetings and responding to emails. He felt shocked at himself that the right choice was even up for debate. That piercing moment of self-awareness would stay with him for the rest of his life.

When we examine how we spend our time, we often overlook meaning and instead focus on the economic value of time. If we can put economic value to the side or even eliminate it from the factors we consider, we're better able to gain insight into how we spend our time and see whether our choices are connected to what matters most to us. It can be our own moment of clarity. I'm spending my time—but am I spending it well?

Ask yourself:
- Do your daily activities align with your priorities?
- Does where you spend your time bring you a sense of fulfillment?

- Does where you spend your time grow relationships?
- Do you spend time on self-care?
- Do you feel satisfied with your day?

THINK AND DISCUSS (PART THREE)

- Do you spend time on what you believe you're supposed to spend time on?
- How do you know you're succeeding?
- Where can you help others be intentional with how they best use their time?
- Are you able to "just be" in the moment, truly be present, and not concern yourself with what's next?

The hardest part of owning your time is being what some people might call selfish. But it's about being self-aware and self-directed.

After all, you and only you can see the totality of your life and what matters most to you. Only you can choose to say yes or no when people make requests—or demands—for your time. And while you probably want to be the nice, helpful, friendly, go-to person, if the actions being asked for don't align with where you want to spend your time, then you must be comfortable saying no. Not "Sorry, no." There's nothing to be sorry for. You're simply choosing to do something else with your time.

Discovering the ability to say no is often easier than finding your current intent or purpose. Feeling confident that we're spending time fulfilling your highest purposes does come. But the journey begins with consciously watching how your time comes and goes, then embracing the opportunity to be intentional and self-directed. With practice, you will be able to own how you spend your time.

CHAPTER 19

Rest, Refresh, and Rejuvenate

I THOUGHT I WAS MASTER OF MY LIFE, MY TIME, AND MY BODY. SO MUCH SO THAT I SIGNED UP FOR AN ALL-OUT PHYSICAL CHALLENGE, ASSUMING I COULD CONTROL EVERY VARIABLE AND ACHIEVE THE AWESOME OUTCOME I ANTICIPATED.

My friend Joe asked if I wanted to join him in a race. Not exactly a race but more of a four-hour structured activity with participants traversing more than 14 miles broken up by three dozen physical challenges. It was basically an obstacle course for grown-ups. I like long-distance challenges, and after doing some research on what it would take to train for this one, I agreed to join Joe on this six-month adventure.

We mapped out our training plan. Most days, we would train separately, and on specific weekends, we would train together for the obstacles. One obstacle was carrying a five-gallon bucket filled with rocks for half a mile. Another was to cross a mud pit on monkey bars. I hadn't been on monkey bars since I was a kid! Yet there we were, one Saturday morning at a playground, two middle-aged guys looking completely stupid trying to complete the once-easy challenge.

After five months of training, my ankles hurt. Not an "ugh, my ankles are sore." One day, I got up and they hurt so bad I could barely walk. I swallowed some painkillers, stretched, took a hot shower, and stretched some more. The pain eased but didn't go away. With just a few weeks to go, I needed to power through the pain and find a way to do the race. I took more pain meds so that I wouldn't waste the months-long training regimen.

On race day, my ankles still hurt. Bad. More pain meds. And more during the race. When we finished, the pain was so bad I collapsed at the finish line and had to be helped to a bench, then to our car. I was truly lucky—and am still extremely grateful—that I didn't develop a long-term injury or even cause permanent damage by powering through. My race time was terrible. My experience was awful. I felt like I wasted a lot of time, effort, and money to do something halfway while putting myself in a position that could have resulted in very serious harm.

THINK AND DISCUSS (PART ONE)

- What parts of your life are in your control?
- What feels out of your control?
- What is actually in your control?
- What is actually out of your control?

Our lives are jammed up. At work, we go nonstop. At home, every evening is filled with things to do, and weekends are packed with errands, activities, and hobbies.

Our activity level seems to reflect our society's high value on being busy. It's the image we value and the image we want to project. By chasing busyness, we often bump into the reality that while some things may be within our control, many things feel way beyond our control. And when things feel out of control, we spiral. When the spiral happens quickly, we often catch it. When the out-of-control feeling builds slowly over time, it can be very difficult for us to spot and correct.

What is actually within our control? Very little. Consider this list:
- Your thoughts, feelings (sort of), and actions
- How you care for yourself (sort of, depending on where you live and

your resources)
- Your goals (as allowed and supported by your surroundings)
- Your effort (unless your environment prevents good sleep and eating habits)
- Your boundaries (again, limited by your environment)
- The way you treat others
- Who you spend time with (sort of)

That's a bit disappointing. Many items on the list should be in our control, but actually aren't. One of the toughest facts to accept is that a significant portion of our lives isn't in our control. Ever been unexpectedly stopped by a train on the way to an important appointment? How about traveling for work, where it can be very challenging to eat right and get good sleep? What about setting boundaries—can you really eliminate that toxic family member from your life?

The illusion of control is just that. While we want...need...and at times are desperate for control, the truth is that almost nothing is fully within our control. Want proof? Consider this list:
- People (you have zero control over people, no matter your title, position, or authority level, including how they act, think, feel, or treat you)
- The weather (you can't reliably predict it, much less control it)
- Time (you can't slow it down or get any more)
- Death (morbid yet true)
- Physical needs of nutrition and rest (sleep and everything else)
- The past (you can't rewrite your own history)
- The future (try as you may, you can't control it)

That's a bit disheartening. In the big picture, there seems like to be nothing much we can do about anything. But check the first item of that first list. Above all else, you can indeed control what comes out from inside yourself—your thoughts, feelings, and actions. (I say "sort of" about feelings because sometimes you're surprised, startled, or forced unexpectedly into a situation where your subconscious takes over, like when you jump out of the way of a speeding car. (I hope you get through life without having to test that statement, but you get my point.) For 99% of our lives, we control our attitudes and what the world around us experiences.

Why consider what is in and out of your control? When we put effort into what is truly within our control and also acknowledge that we are mere humans who can't power through everything (I'll sleep when I'm dead!), then we can see and act on real opportunities to better care for ourselves and those around us.

Consider Jerry, a guy who just wouldn't and couldn't stop. When he wasn't at work, he was on the go, filling his days with things to do. When I asked him how he rested, he stared at me blankly, and in a very serious tone, he said, "I don't." For more than sixty years, he's never been able to rest. His career elevated him to positions where he needed to be in control, as the business depended on execution at a high level. And it carried over into the rest of his life. On his vacations, he climbed mountains. Literally. Like Kilimanjaro. When others would encourage him to take a break, sit back, relax, and enjoy life, he looked at them the same way he looked at me—with a confused and dumbfounded look that said, "We're given limited time on this Earth, why in the world would you waste it resting?"

Why can't Jerry rest? Does Jerry ever feel the need to rejuvenate himself? Is Jerry even capable of refreshing himself—his body, mind, or soul? And what gives with other people at the other extreme—who easily find time to just lie around and never break a sweat?

Let's look at definitions of three terms:

- **Rest:** An instance or period of relaxing or ceasing to engage in strenuous or stressful activity.
- **Refresh:** To give new strength or energy to; to reinvigorate.
- **Rejuvenate:** To give new energy or vigor to; to revitalize.

In the TED article "The 7 Types of Rest That Every Person Needs," Dr. Saundra Dalton-Smith writes about the variety of **rest** you require for your own well-being:

1. **Physical rest.** Passive physical rest is sleeping and napping, while active physical rest includes yoga, stretching, taking long walks, and light exercise.
2. **Mental rest.** You know, when you try to sleep and just keep thinking about deadlines? Or you can't let go of your list of to-dos for the kids? Or the times you wake up feeling like you didn't sleep at all? These indicate

you need mental rest. Vacations and time off can help, though you need to find ways in between those large breaks to find ways to mentally disengage. Like engaging in a hobby, gaming, or journaling—activities that require all your focus.

3. **Sensory rest.** We've somehow become okay with allowing multiple ways for people to reach us—phone, text, email, instant message, messaging apps, work-specific instant messages. When these come at us in high volume, we can easily get sensory overload from technology. Anything we can do to disengage momentarily from the over-stimulation will allow us to feel sensory rest.

4. **Creative rest.** If you're like Jerry—constantly solving problems, creating new ideas, or seeking things to do—creative rest can be very powerful. Others don't experience this as rest. Hobbies like painting, photography, writing, playing video games, and building models allow some people to engage in activities where they get things done yet engage their body and brain differently from their normal routines. This type of rest can allow you to disassociate and become consumed by the creative activity.

5. **Emotional rest.** If you're a caregiver by nature or career (or both), you understand the need for emotional rest. People with high levels of empathy are pushed each day as they connect and take on the emotional burdens of others. Teachers, nurses, and counselors are examples of those who must find places to get emotional rest.

6. **Social rest.** If you attend work conferences and long to escape to your hotel room for alone time, you understand social rest. While others may enjoy and even rest by engaging with other people, too much social interaction can exhaust people who are not naturally wired for it. And if the nature of your social interactions is draining, then your need to remove yourself and to capture rest outside of social environments becomes even more important.

7. **Spiritual rest.** Prayer, meditation, spiritual enlightenment, and engagement with spiritual and faith-based communities will allow you to gain spiritual rest. This rest allows you to connect to feel a deep sense of belonging, acceptance, and explore purpose.

Get it? Sleep isn't the only rest you need.

You also require **refreshment**—gaining new strength or energy, or put another way, "reinvigorating."

If the goal of refreshing is finding new energy, then you must first recognize and let yourself be okay with feeling low on energy and strength. Life wears you down. Admit it! To hit a wall during the day when your physical and/or mental energy is spent happens to all of us. You are not a failure, and there is no shame. To look forward to sitting on the couch after dinner or collapsing into bed is normal.

We need to counter society's "do more" and "do everything" mentality that makes us feel like failures when we run out of gas. Consider the book The 10X Rule, which says, "You must set targets that are 10 times what you think you want and then do 10 times what you think it will take to accomplish those targets." Oh my. If you want more, just do more. That works for a while. Until it costs you things like health and friends.

Then what are some concrete ways to refresh? In the ideas below, you'll notice overlap with strategies for rest. But consider how each of these activities resonates with you. Do they cause you to power down (rest) or to power up (refresh)?

- **Physical activity:** Go for a walk, run, exercise, stretch
- **Go outside:** Get fresh air and sunshine
- **Mindfulness practices:** Meditation, deep breathing, and intentionally trying to slow your thinking
- **Nutrition and hydration:** Eat well and drink plenty of water
- **Sensory input:** Listen to music, enjoy nature sounds, smell something pleasant like mints or outdoor air, and find ways to engage in human touch
- **Social:** Spend time with friends and family
- **Creative outlets:** Read, draw, listen to music, or game
- **Avoid social media:** Do I need to explain that?
- **Pause and celebrate yourself:** Even if you feel like no one else does!

Rejuvenation means to gain new energy or revitalize. Have you ever trained physically for something for so long that you lost interest? Or stayed in the same job doing the same thing that it became so rote that if anyone suggested a better way to do the work, you couldn't even entertain their idea? At some point, the fire dies out, your passion fades, and what used to excite and invigorate you is gone. Once again—admit it! These are sure signs you need to rediscover the energy, passion, and dedication that you started with. Perhaps you need to act on what used to push you. Dig for the passion that once fueled your soul, seek a new passion, and act to rejuvenate that interest and seriously pursue it.

THINK AND DISCUSS (PART TWO)

- What prevents you from:
  - Resting?
  - Refreshing?
  - Rejuvenating?
- How can you intentionally find time to:
  - Rest?
  - Refresh
  - Rejuvenate

We can all find many reasons (excuses?) to not allow ourselves the time for all three modes of recovery and recharge—rest, refresh, and rejuvenate. Each is essential.

In practice, rejuvenation is a larger, longer endeavor, a combination of physical, mental, and spiritual.

Taylor always wanted to visit Moab, Utah, a place with countless opportunities for outdoor activities. Life got in the way, and before he knew it, Taylor's youngest kid was leaving for college. Suddenly finding fewer constraints on his time, he took a week to himself and headed to Moab. Taylor was good at his job and was trying to figure out what to do next, and he decided a week in the high desert would be a nice break. He didn't intend to find a new direction in life at this moment, though that's exactly what happened.

Taylor intentionally disconnected for the week, opting for his tent rather than a hotel. He turned off his phone. Rather than planning ahead, he pulled into town and looked for available campsites. He found a spot, set up his tent, and headed to the city's visitor center for a lay of the land. The helpful folks there sold him a couple of maps and advised where to hike, bike, and drive. Taylor was surprised yet strangely happy with this "take it as it comes" approach.

Over many days, Taylor explored the area. He met many people on the trails, each with fascinating stories to share. At one point, he was hiking one of the most remote trails in Arches National Park. As he paused to sit and sip some water, he looked up and was overcome with the silence. Growing up and working in a large city for most of his life, he had never been to a place this remote. Not a person was in sight. Not a plane in the sky. Without any wind, it was complete and total silence. Taylor had never heard silence like this. Once he noticed it, he was in wonder. For many moments, Taylor was overcome. He felt something. Time stopped. He was one with the world.

A few days later, Taylor wandered up another recommended trail, this time into the Blue Mountains. As he hiked toward a pass, he noticed the changes in ecosystems. First high desert, then forest, then high forest filled with aspens, and finally he crossed the timberline, so high up that nothing grew. When he reached the pass, a saddle formation between two peaks, he could suddenly see for miles in two directions. The awesomeness of this view left him awestruck, and afterwards, he couldn't recall how long he spent on that pass.

As the week drew to a close, Taylor began thinking about his career. While he wasn't sure what was next, he knew inside that going back to the same work was no longer in the cards. He wasn't sure why that was, though he was absolutely sure of it. He felt an energy, a drive, a sudden feeling that propelled him to no longer engage in the work he had been doing for so long. His time away, resting his mind and refreshing his body, allowed him to experience a rejuvenation, where he found new energy to seek out what he was going to do next.

THINK AND DISCUSS (PART THREE)

How can you ensure both you and those around you find time to intentionally develop space and habits to...

- Rest?
- Refresh?
- Rejuvenate?

I had a lot of time to think before, during, and after my bad race day. I was mad at myself for both overexerting and underperforming,

I came to realize that I had to control what I could control and let go of the rest. If I could train hard while simultaneously remaining healthy, I could do better. In fact, way better.

That thought slowly became a hard, then healthy, and finally, a happy challenge. For weeks, I backed way off doing anything physical until I got to the point where I could walk pain-free. Then I started training again. Slowly. Listening carefully to my body. After a few months, I was in good shape, and the nudge came up inside me that said to go try another race. Do it again, this time healthy. So I did. I needed rest to heal, refresh to consider the possibility of another race, and rejuvenation to thrive in my second attempt.

When we have experiences that prompt us to recognize the importance of all three—rest, refresh, and rejuvenate—then we can help others first recognize they too need to practice and experience them. We must weave the conversations of rest, refresh, and rejuvenation into our daily conversations with those around us regularly for our and their health, wellness, and well-being.

CHAPTER 20

———

Purpose

LIVE WITH PURPOSE. WORK WITH PURPOSE. FIND YOUR PURPOSE! EXPECTATIONS ABOUT LIVING WITH MEANING AND FULFILLMENT ARE ALL AROUND US.

A healthcare organization wants to help you "live a healthier life." A financial services company pitches services with a promise to help you "retire well." A soda company claims to "refresh the world and make a difference."

Are these slogans for real? Our inner cynic suspects that corporate mission, vision, and purpose statements are little more than marketing spin, nice words the organization puts out to get us to buy more stuff. Does anyone really believe that drinking carbonated sugar water will change the world?

What about individuals? Not your company, position, or role—just you. Do you have a purpose? How confident are you about your answer?

My brother always knew what he wanted to do with his life. Among other details, his purpose included the industry he wanted to work in. Me? I wandered for years after school, often having no idea what I wanted to do or where I wanted to work. As I said many times during that period, "I don't know what I'm supposed to do with my life—right now or overall." Life loomed huge, and with many years ahead of me, the search for long-term purpose overwhelmed me. In the meantime, I needed money for food and rent. I just needed a job.

At first, I tried to figure out what kind of job would be meaningful for me and the world. But choosing a job that would positively impact the entire planet and its people is a lofty expectation. I asked myself how I would recognize purposeful work when I found it. Would it make me externally successful? Fulfill me internally? Put me in a role where I could help others? All the above?

Being young and single, my circumstances shaped my search for purpose. I didn't know what I was looking for, but I did have enormous freedom to explore. As I hunted for my answer, more thoughts occurred to me. Maybe I should look for a job as a means to an end—a gig to support a higher purpose outside of work—although I still had no idea what might be. And I still wondered if, once I figured that out, would everything still be up in the air? What would I do after that?

THINK AND DISCUSS (PART ONE)

1. Do you know your purpose? For right now? For your life?
2. How have you searched for purpose? How have you found it?
3. Do you chase purpose or let it come to you?
4. Are you achieving or living your purpose right now? How do you know?

What you do each day at work might bring you purpose. Or not.

The dictionary definition of purpose is straightforward. Purpose is the reason for which something is done or created, or the reason it exists. All you need to do is articulate why you were created and the reason you exist. No sweat!

Another definition lowers the stakes.1 Purpose is what we have as our intention or objective. Let's focus on this more doable definition.

When you set a goal, you state a metric or another definition that signals when you've achieved it. Suppose you want to run a half-marathon. That's 13.2 miles of running. Perhaps you want to run a sub-two-hour time, or maybe you simply want to finish. You set the goal, gain moral support by telling your friends, craft your training plan, pick the day you will run the distance, and begin. According to the definition, you now have a purpose.

What about your work? Some jobs require people to write annual goals.

Like "Over the next year, I will increase sales by 30%." "I will increase production by 15%." "I will improve our team engagement level by 40%." You state the outcome and the measurement.

Do goals create a sense of purpose in our work? Is that all there is to it?

Some jobs have outcomes that feel harder to quantify, but they seem to have an obvious immediate purpose, such as teaching, nursing, or caring for the elderly. Other roles aren't so altruistic, but they have concrete outcomes, like the grocery store stocker who can see directly how her work helps others, or the maintenance technician who replaces light bulbs at a government building.

Does your position give you purpose? Or can the mission of an organization give you purpose?

Simon Sinek's book and TED Talk "Start with Why" make the case that people are loyal to companies because of the company's *why*, that is, its purpose. He uses Apple as a case study, demonstrating that Apple is an anti-corporate company that exists to create things for rebels. Products that lean into this brand, combined with fierce customer loyalty, have made Apple successful. Moreover, Apple's purpose has always been clear: its products and services are for people who want to leverage technology to challenge the status quo. It's said that Apple employees live and breathe this purpose.

Do you have strong feelings about where you buy car tires? I do.

I first went to a Les Schwab tire store because I could walk home while they worked on my car, and a quick online search showed decent prices and quality tire brands. A few months later, I woke up one morning to a flat caused by driving over a nail. I jacked up the car, threw the flat tire in our other car, and headed to Les Schwab. As I was parking, a guy walked out to my car and took my info, and I went inside to wait. Five minutes later, he said my tire was ready to go. Because I was already a customer in their system, the fix was free.

Years later, I needed tires for another car. I went back to Les Schwab. The process seemed to take forever, as mechanics took the car on three test drives, which lasted well past the shop's closing time. The manager finally informed me there was a noise coming from under the car, and they couldn't figure out what it was. He took me for a test drive, and I was able to hear the noise. He recommended a local mechanic, who was able to look at the car the next day.

My brand loyalty is tied to why. I can state with deep confidence that Les Schwab's purpose is customer service. Everything they do revolves around ensuring customers have a positive experience worth coming back for.

I have noticed an entirely different reasoning for buying online, where my purchasing decisions are driven by price and reviews. When I shop for groceries, I go to two different chains because I know they have different items on sale. And when I buy a TV, my purchase is all about price, reviews, and availability. I don't care about the why of the company that makes it. In fact, I can't tell you the brand of the last TV I bought.

I enjoy going to Les Schwab because their purpose as a company is exemplified through their people. The employees know their stuff, are incessantly helpful, and go above and beyond my expectations. But while the company's purpose is clear, does that give each employee a satisfying sense of purpose?

Does purpose matter in the organization you work for? Does it impact you? Or is the purpose unique to you?

THINK AND DISCUSS (PART TWO)

1. Does your purpose change over time? Does your purpose change at various moments in time or seasons of life? Does your lifelong purpose change?
2. How could you define your purpose at work or home, in your family, or as a leader, parent, or friend? Do your whys overlap? How are they similar? Do they conflict?
3. When do you experience your purposes in various roles battling for your time?
4. Once you achieve a short-term purpose—like achieving a goal or making a small life change—what happens?

Finding purpose can be elusive. Once you find it, you might achieve it. Or your purpose might no longer fulfill you, so you reexamine, revise, or abandon it.

The half-marathon is a few weeks away. You trained for twelve weeks, feeling simultaneously awful yet great along the way. You feel like you've already accomplished something major, and now your goal is within reach. You spend two weeks tapering before the big day. The day comes, and you complete your run. You accomplished your goal.

Have you fulfilled your purpose? Now what?

Perhaps you pause and enjoy the moment. Or you start planning for a full marathon. Or maybe you quit running and join a pickleball league. Now that you've achieved your purpose, chances are good you'll want a new goal or purpose to pursue.

What about a purpose for life? That's an enormous question, perhaps best left up to philosophers, religion, and the spiritual realm. But for many of us, the question finds its way into our lives from time to time.

Changes and challenges in the seasons of our lives often bring purpose. The sudden layoff of a spouse may require focus on tightening finances while supporting the transition of job loss, followed by a search. A new child's arrival will require less sleep, more work, and a thoughtful reallocation of your time. Enjoying a house full of teenagers could require a lot more driving, events, and parental assistance with short- and long-term goals.

These all bring a purpose to your life for a season. You sort of sign up for these, although it's a more significant choice than a half-marathon.

Can an overarching life purpose come from work? Sometimes. Will purpose at work come and go? Probably.

Have you experienced a time when everyone came together, put in the extra work, went above and beyond, and crossed the finish line together?

Sometimes those meaningful moments happen in a single day, like when a new restaurant opens and the entire staff comes together to make opening night a success. Other moments span months, like when a new school must be built in less than a year before the building welcomes its first students. These one-time events can bring purpose through urgency, focus, and clear objectives.

These events can be opportunities to find meaning at work. Consider Stan, who launched a career in architecture and found his way into a large organization that purchased architectural services. After ten years in an organization, he was thrust into leading two very large projects. These projects went on for several years, and their size and impact on the company brought plenty of attention. Wherever he went, he was the center of attention. He embraced the purpose of delivering these two projects.

Then the projects finished. Suddenly, he was without purpose. There were no large projects on the horizon, and his role was significantly reduced. Within a few months, he left the organization. His personal purpose was driven by the complexity and recognition that came with the large projects, and without that, his purpose at work evaporated.

For some, their purpose at work may rise and fall with goals and projects. Others find fulfillment in day-to-day "consistent persistence." An elementary school teacher may have a longer goal to survive the school year, yet find daily fulfillment when kids do well, when they find joy in learning, or make progress on difficult subjects.

What happens when your work purpose runs headlong into your personal purpose? When Stan took on the large projects and found himself needing to work longer hours, for example, his family saw him less, and his purpose as a dad and husband had to take a back seat. He decided that for a season, the two large projects had to be his priority. When gymnast Simone Biles stepped out of Olympic competition for mental health reasons, her personal purpose of wellness took priority over even the highest levels of competition.

When we have clarified our purposes, do we communicate where we are heading with those around us? Do we share our purpose?

THINK AND DISCUSS (PART THREE)

1. Do each of us have a purpose? Is purpose unique to each of us, or is there an overlap with the purposes of others?
2. How do you know your purpose is correct?
3. How do you react when you're in a season where you feel purposeless?
4. How can you help others walk through seasons when they struggle to find purpose?

When we lack purpose in any aspect of our lives, we're often awash with a multitude of emotions. Those feelings can undo us, or they can motivate us to find a way forward.

Without purpose, intent, objectives, and goals, life can feel dull or even empty. Yet pausing and feeling a lack of purpose can be helpful, and dedicating time to reflection, searching, and exploration can turn out to be very healthy.

How can you notice when people in your orbit lack a sense of purpose? How does that absence of meaning show up in their words, expressions, and behavior? How can you recognize their state, and what steps can you take to do something for or with them?

When you have purpose—work or personal, life-long or seasonal—you feel good. You have intent, a way to live each day that moves you toward your goals and to live more in tune with your purpose. When you're in this state, people may notice you're happier, more driven, focused, going up instead of down, and in a better overall state.

Rather than making people wonder why you're this way, what would happen if you told them? Others are in that same good place, looking to be in it, or frustrated they aren't. Take a moment and share with them the purpose you're working on and why you find it fulfilling.

CHAPTER 21

———

Belief

BELIEFS SHAPE OUR THOUGHTS, GUIDE OUR BEHAVIORS, AND INFLUENCE HOW WE INTERPRET OUR EXPERIENCES. OUR BELIEFS FORM EARLY.

Growing up in Chicago, I spent Sundays at my grandmother's house. Six grown children with families of their own added up to a big family with huge gatherings of uncles, aunts, and cousins, plus neighborhood friends. We often went straight to grandma's from Sunday mass, staying for the afternoon and sometimes well into the evening. My earliest memories are playing running bases with cousins, and as I got older, I began to eavesdrop on kitchen table conversations, where grown-ups discussed the latest issues. The new Chicago mayor. Various aldermen and district politics. The new priest at church. Neighborhood decline. The Polish community spreading thin.

I looked up to these adults. They were smart, engaged, and passionate. And they were family. My beliefs that formed in those years included:

1. Chicago mayors all screw up the city, except for Mayor Daley—the father, not the no-good son.
2. Our deeply rooted Catholic faith was correct.
3. Education will get you far.
4. Work hard and never ask for raises or promotions.
5. Family is the most important.

6. Getting together as a family on holidays is expected.
7. The Detroit Pistons basketball team were the enemy.

As I entered high school and beyond, I carried these beliefs with me. Like most people in their teens and early twenties, I began to expand my thinking, meet people with divergent beliefs, and internally either reinforce or modify my inherited belief systems. As my experiences broadened, some tenets formed by what others said or what I inferred began to soften. Other beliefs I had formed in childhood from my parents, teachers, mentors, and friends became my own absolutes.

When I read *Boss* by Mike Royko, my beliefs about Mayor Daley changed. Taking a course in college about the Bible as a literary work enlightened my beliefs about the Catholic Church. Personal experiences of being skipped for promotions due to my lack of self-advocacy impacted my belief around how people get raises. No matter what I experienced, the Pistons continued to be the enemy.

Of course, this process isn't the same for everybody. Some kids develop their own beliefs right from the start, regardless of what others tell them to believe. Other parents and kids are natural opposites, like a parent who believes that hard work and study lead to a fruitful life, and clashes with a free-thinking kid more in tune with art and music. Or a parent who drinks and smokes may raise a child resolutely against both for a multitude of reasons.

As we move through life, our beliefs develop from what we're taught by people we trust, mixed with what we retrofit through our experiences, expansion of knowledge, and our own conclusions. In our adult lives, beliefs become deeply held assumptions and convictions about ourselves, others, and the world around us. They shape what we see and do and help us make sense of our circumstances. These beliefs inform our expectations of ourselves, our expectations of others, and our judgments of others.

THINK AND DISCUSS (PART ONE)

- What are your core beliefs? What enduring and unwavering beliefs guide you?
- What influenced and crafted your belief system?

- Where have you had such a strong belief that no one could stop you?
- When have you made decisions based on your beliefs?

People with a high sense of belief know where they stand and let others know. Others hold their beliefs inside, yet are no less motivated by their convictions.

CliftonStrengths identifies people with the Belief theme as having strong, unchanging core values. It states, "These values vary from one person to another, but ordinarily your Belief theme causes you to be family-oriented, altruistic, even spiritual, and to value responsibility and high ethics—both in yourself and others."

People with strong beliefs must find meaningful work that matters to them as individuals and makes room for them to live out their personal values. They are seen as passionate, steadfast, altruistic, family-oriented, ethical, and responsible. For example, they will still track their hours even in a salaried position, they expect people to be present during "normal" work hours, and they may see the world as black and white, which includes clear right and wrong.

How about people who seldom outwardly display any strong beliefs? Do they lack faith in themselves or in what they think? Maybe—or maybe not!

Annette was an up-and-coming star who came into her role as a project assistant seemingly out of nowhere. From her beginnings in manufacturing, she wanted a change and found one in a nearby university, where she helped deliver large projects with a multitude of components. She assisted with designs, ordered materials, and coordinated work to get projects over the finish line. After a brief orientation period, she felt comfortable and was well respected by her team and internal clients.

When a project manager suddenly left the university, Annette didn't show any reaction. That same day, her boss asked Annette if she was planning to apply for the open position. She immediately declined. Her boss let that response hang for a moment. Annette wasn't sure what to do, but she was certain she wasn't ready to take on the project management role. Was the boss serious? She felt uneasy, yet believed in her gut the right answer was no. She was surprised when the boss said, "Well, you should." Then he got up and left.

Annette pondered this. She was absolutely steadfast in her assessment that she wasn't ready. As she reassured herself that she was correct to not pursue the job, her boss asked her coworkers if they thought she was ready. Overwhelmingly, the response was yes. Team members, internal staff, and external vendors all had the same reaction: "She's ready." "She can do this." "We've got her back." "We'll help her succeed." The next day, the boss shared with Annette what he had heard. He asked again if she would apply. After hearing all the feedback, Annette said, "Well, I guess I have to after all the nice things people said about me!"

Believing in yourself as a person isn't necessarily the same as believing that you can accomplish something. Annette always trusted in her ability to reach goals she set for herself, but at first, she didn't believe she was qualified for this specific job.

You might find yourself in the same place as Annette. You may struggle from time to time to convince yourself of your abilities. Doubt exists when you think others have weighed in against you. However, your belief system may still allow for the setting of personal goals and achieving them in spite of the doubt created by external forces. Running a marathon. Writing a book. Volunteering in the community.

Perhaps your belief system is rooted in a philosophy of "If I build it, they will come." If you study, work hard, and develop yourself, you will get promoted. If you put in the time and effort to get into shape, while it may take a long time, you believe good things will result. The outcomes are clear, and you have faith that something will happen.

When I took over leading a large project management group, there were disconnected policies, procedures, processes, and no formal structure for doing business in place. My job was to tie everything together and put it into action.

But I wanted more. I wanted people to feel connected to their work and each other. I wanted lower turnover. I wanted happier employees. Plus, good, positive conflict on our projects where people trusted each other enough to argue passionately and then go get lunch together. Driving everything was my belief that we could deliver our best work if we did it together. I wasn't sure if this belief sprang from my experiences, upbringing, or genetic make-up. I felt a strong inner push to focus on getting people to be intentional about working with each other.

My goal of collaboration met resistance. I heard, "Who needs that? We've completed projects worth hundreds of millions of dollars without this stuff!"

Someone said, "If you act on feedback from vendors, people will think you're getting kickbacks." I agreed with the first point, giving credit for all the good work already completed. I blatantly ignored the second. Even as I heard objections from my boss, colleagues, staff, and vendors, my internal belief system didn't waver.

THINK AND DISCUSS (PART TWO)

- Where have strong beliefs steered you right?
- Where have strong beliefs steered you wrong?
- When have your beliefs caused you to get tunnel vision?
- Which of your beliefs have shifted over time—or completely changed?

When your beliefs are overly strong, people can experience you as stubborn, set in your ways, elitist, immune to other ideas, and overly opinionated.

This unintended reaction happened, ironically, on my journey for our team to be collaborative! As I learned more and more about people-centric business models, I became even more entrenched in my belief that it was the way we should exist. The benefits, outcomes, organizational impacts, the positives for individuals and teams—all the signs, learning, methods, examples, and study led me to strengthen my belief that this was where we needed to go. And we needed to go there right away. Immediately. Yesterday. I became so absorbed with this concept and its promised outcome that others began to experience all the challenges of working for someone with overly strong beliefs. I was stubborn. I became short-tempered with people who questioned the direction. People who knew me said I was passionate, though that was a kind way to say, "He's being arrogant again. Ignore him."

My operating mode quickly became, "I know what I'm doing, where we're going, and you need to get on board. I believe in this. You should, too." What I overlooked was the need to acknowledge that other people didn't share my strong belief in this journey, and no matter how right I might be, I needed to exercise self-awareness and patience. Shear force wouldn't get them to believe. Believe me, I tried a lot of force! I was so convinced of the power of collaboration that I was blind to the needs of the very people I was trying to collaborate with.

Once a belief takes hold of you, how does it change? For example, how does someone move from believing leadership is all about dispensing answers from on high to a servant leadership style? How does a person go from being raised in organized religion to living as an agnostic? How does an individual shift from altruistic ethics to bending the rules and looking the other way for self-preservation and self-gain?

It turns out our environments have a lot to do with our beliefs. Take Steve, who, early in his career, was an aspiring architect. He was outgoing, personable, and enjoyed his profession. As the years went by, he got married, had a few kids, moved up in responsibility at work, and all the expected things. One day, an old friend from his early career ran into him. Steve was happy to see him and was excited to catch up over lunch. During their meal, with the obligatory niceties out of the way, his friend asked about the conferences and association meetings Steve's team was engaged with. Steve immediately jumped into his last three personal presentations. His friend laughed and said, "Same old Steve! Still only focused on yourself!"

Steve was taken aback. He had known no other way! His boss always talked about himself, and the company he worked for seemed to embrace this self-focused approach. Steve was always the center of attention. He enjoyed the focus on him and his performance. The company even rewarded this behavior. Why would his old friend challenge him like this?

How do you change beliefs? Challenge them, modify them, swap them—it's hard. Beliefs are resistant to change. Visualization and affirmations can help. Experience, particularly bad experiences, can impact your mind's readiness to change. When your belief causes harm to you or those you love, it can prompt you to seriously question your beliefs. That can be true on many fronts, but let's focus on our personal beliefs about how we act, behave, lead, work with others, parent, and live out our ethics.

Steve was challenged by his friend about his approach to his focus on himself. He was successful and well compensated for being what others recognized as self-centered. He began to search inside and realize that while he had proven himself more than capable of living this way, an inner voice began to rumble that his approach may no longer be suited to this time of his life. Perhaps he could find others to present instead of him, giving others the stage. Steve didn't believe they would do nearly as good as he could—he didn't change THAT much THAT fast—but the voice inside kept whispering that perhaps he didn't always have to be "the guy."

Perhaps we, too, have friends who can point out where our beliefs are holding us back. Or maybe when we're in a quiet, peaceful state, we hear voices that question how we approach situations and people in our lives. Perhaps our spouse, kids, or parents are speaking truth, yet our currently held beliefs are causing us not to listen. Perhaps, like Steve, our environments reinforce beliefs that may be in tension with our deep-down beliefs.

THINK AND DISCUSS (PART THREE)

- How are your beliefs currently helping you thrive? Holding you back?
- How are your environments reinforcing or challenging your beliefs?
- When have you believed in others when they didn't believe in themselves?
- Where and how can you believe in others who don't have faith in themselves?

Beliefs can cause failure. Or breakthroughs. It's all about holding tight to accurate beliefs and adjusting those that let us down.

I was interviewing for a job and faced a typical HR question: "What's one of your faults?" I paused for a minute, then confidently answered, "I believe in people." Silence. The interviewer, a seasoned professional who helped start the company I was trying to work for, gave me a quizzical look and said, "Tell me about that." I shared two stories where I hired people for jobs that were way out of their abilities. I believed that with the right people, the right support, and the right attitudes, anything was possible. And I got burnt. Twice. The interviewers asked if I still believe in people. I said I did. Those experiences hadn't jaded or weakened my belief in people. I shared that my solution was to ensure my belief in people was coupled with reality, hope, and ambition.

Belief in others can make great things happen. One of the best team members I have ever worked with wanted to return to school. As an active parent in a document processing role, her aspiration of obtaining a bachelor's degree was a smart next step for her career and her family, but she didn't believe she could do it. The time, the cost, the impact on work—all kinds of things right in front of her were screaming, "No way! This isn't you! You're not capable! You're not worthy!" We talked for months about this dilemma, and I encouraged her to share with the team the challenges she believed that going back to school would create. She needed two or more years of flex schedule. She feared letting down so many people!

As this woman talked to the team members, she was overwhelmed by the encouragement and the belief that she had the power, talent, support, and ability to go do this. What about our work? The team responded that they would figure it out. How? "Together." When the day came to commit, she did it. With the team's belief in her that she could do it, she took the first step. And many more. Was it challenging? Yes. Did the team ever falter in their belief that this was undeniably the right thing for her to do? No. Not once. Never.

By the way, Annette got the job. She thrived in the position she at first believed she wasn't qualified for.

Belief in others, from one person or from many, can transform lives. Who needs to hear about your belief in them right now?

CHAPTER 22

Hope

HOPE: THE BELIEF THAT THE FUTURE WILL BE BETTER THAN THE PRESENT. AND TAKING ACTION TO GET THERE.

Coming into a large organization from a modest family-owned business was a big change for Kelly. During the interview process, she was excited to discover all the good things she could make great. Processes needed to be revamped, relationships with the community could be improved, and internal departmental relationships required mending. She was fired up, eager for the challenge, and poised to hit the ground running.

As her two-year work anniversary neared, Kelly walked a ten-year veteran of the organization through her efforts, noting the resistance she repeatedly met. Charlie listened as Kelly recounted repeatedly overcoming one hurdle only to have ten more pop up. Or winning over key employees and watching them take jobs elsewhere. Even when she had all the buy-in necessary to implement a change, random departments like Risk, Legal, or Compliance would show up with a mighty sigh and tell her to hold up. She now realized that was code for "This isn't going to happen."

When Charlie asked how Kelly felt, she replied that she understood why people come and go from this company—it's impossible to make a difference! "You lasted longer than most," he said. "I remember the day when each member of our team realized that trying hard—like you—isn't worth it. We just saw you completely and utterly lose all hope."

Have you ever started a new job or relocated to a new place, fully expecting it to be great? All you see is a dazzling future with endless opportunities.

Optimism is a belief that things will work out—that they will get better. Hope is more. It's an active feeling and mindset that achieving your goals will require work to overcome challenges, whether environmental, circumstantial, or internal. Hope is driven by both emotion and thinking. The emotional component is your trust in receiving and extending care rooted in relationships with people and the world in general. The thinking part is your will and drive to obtain your desired outcome.

THINK AND DISCUSS (PART ONE)

- Where in your life do you have hope?
- How do you define hope? How might you tweak that definition for home? At work?
- When has hope positively impacted your life?
- Where have you felt hope fade away?

Why is hope important in our lives?

Hope matters. It motivates us for the future, provides a reason to work toward goals, and assures us there's something better ahead for us, whether that's emotional resilience, physical well-being, mental accomplishments, or achieving goals.

Think of all the people and resources that support your sense of hope. For me, family clearly tops my list. My parents, wife, and kids all exert the strongest positive influence in my life. In fact, I would say at least one family member significantly impacts me each day.

At work, however, I rarely experience that degree of impact. Only in my early frontline jobs did I have daily interactions with my boss. As leaders get farther away organizationally—VP, SVP, CEO—our interactions are almost exclusively one-way. They tell us what we need to know and do through technology. And while books, history, and studies impact the hope I have inside of me, they don't give me the level of hope I get from my family each day.

The 2025 World Governments Summit, in collaboration with Gallup, created the "Global Leadership Report: What Followers Want." Surveying 30,000 people across 52 countries, the study found that people's greatest need from their leaders is hope. Trust is second, followed by compassion and stability. Here's how the study defines the four terms:

1. **Hope:** the need to feel positive about the future and for leaders to provide a clear direction
2. **Trust:** the need for honesty, respect, and integrity
3. **Compassion:** the need to feel cared about and listened to
4. **Stability:** the need for psychological safety and secure foundations during times of uncertainty.

This desire for hope is widespread across all countries and ages. One particularly notable statistic: 56% of all the attributes displayed by impactful leaders concern hope, which is substantially more than the next attribute, trust.

If hope is what we as followers seek from those who lead us—but we don't always get it— can we create hope within ourselves?

What if you went to the doctor and found out you had a serious disease? The doctor says the chances of you beating the disease are 50/50. The optimist would see this glass as half full. The pessimist would see it as half empty and leaking out the bottom.

How would you react? You're suddenly faced with long months of treatments, visits, and costs. Would you be optimistic? Or could you tell yourself to hope for the best and turn that desire into action? Here's what that might look like. You tell yourself, "This is serious. It's not going to be fun. The doctor gave me a path, and if I follow directions and stay on the path, I should be able to come out of this okay."

That's hope! You connect your feeling that something can be accomplished with the mental pathway to get it done. You feel it. And you anticipate experiencing it.

The world does a great job of crushing hope. Many young people enter the workforce not understanding that racism, sexism, and bullying exist in the grown-up world until they discover the reality firsthand. Then there's politics with its never-ending barrage of negativity and news outlets pouring out doomsday-speak. Or the world hits us with the cost of living. Or healthcare, where hope can evaporate in an instant with a confusing test result, a turn in severity, or a heavy statistic that says your chances are slim. And there's that inevitable learning that, like Kelly, no matter how hard you try, you aren't going to make a difference.

THINK AND DISCUSS (PART TWO)

- What do you currently hope for?
- What inspires you to hope?
- Where have you seen hope attempted and fall short?
- Where have you doubted hope, and things turned out well?

What about losing hope? Can we live without it? Have you ever lost hope in yourself, your life, your job, or in humanity? Can you get it back?

The real estate and economic collapse of 2007 devastated my personal hope. Late in the year, as the company I was working with was collapsing, I was interviewing for a promising opportunity with a solid company. I had hope throughout the interview process as each interview took me farther into their hiring process. I traveled to a satellite office, their headquarters, and finally to a company-wide event where I joined the festivities. I hadn't yet received an offer, but I had all the hope in the world that while my family and I would need to relocate, we were going to be okay.

Then a few weeks went by with no communication. No reach out, next step, or contact. My current job came to an end, the company closed, and I was without a job. Another two weeks without any word from the new organization. While my concerns grew, I never lost hope that this was going to work out. Then the phone call came, where I was told they had paused all hiring, including me.

I was stunned. I stepped outside onto my porch and closed the door behind me so my son wouldn't hear the panic in my voice. I almost begged them to hire me, since there were no jobs anywhere and all my job hunting was turning up empty. The person on the other end of the phone ended our conversation as fast as it started. I hung up and stood alone on my porch. Tears in my eyes. An ache in my heart. Totally and utterly hopeless.

I struggled for a while, feeling like my world had just collapsed. I had a tremendous mortgage, a young family, and no job. I always had the ability to turn lemons into lemonade. When I was young, my mom had a tough time punishing me, because when she sent me to my room to discipline me, I would thank her and tell her I had all kinds of toys in there that I hadn't played with in a long time. But losing my job and ultimately my house should have caused me to lose all hope. And for a while, it did.

A few months later, I found myself in a group of unemployed professionals just like me—all without a job and many without hope. I spoke to many people there, as I was actively job hunting and networking the best I could. Many of the group participants were depressed. They were middle-aged, tossed from high-paying jobs that no longer existed, and whatever hope they had was gone. They held a strong belief that life wasn't going to get better. Bills piled up, job application after application went unanswered, and the news each day was bleak, yet for some reason, twice a week, this group got together.

The state employee leading the group did everything she could to help us. Cindy brought in relevant speakers, interview coaches, and skills training. Anything to foster hope. The group's commitment to coming together—along with the acts of getting up, showering, and driving to the gathering—created and reinforced hope within the members. It would have been easy to show up in jeans and T-shirts, yet the group felt a bond in dressing as though they were headed to the office. And a little encouragement from Cindy helped!

From time to time, the group would notice someone was no longer attending, and we hoped that person had found a job. Cindy made it clear each time we got together that this moment in our lives would pass. This experience is temporary. This isn't forever. Members of the group began to believe her statements, and many felt a spark, a rekindling of light that felt buried deep in the darkness. The bond created by the group allowed for hope to ignite and prosper within the members.

Hope was fostered by Cindy in a way that the hope felt as though it came from the collective. We knew we were all in this together, and if we stuck together, we would all get out of it. Cindy was instrumental in helping hundreds of mid-career people get on their feet and back into life. She brought hope day after day. She never wavered. Her belief in the people in the room created and reinforced a strong sense of hope.

I have been a part of many teams, professional and personal, where all hope seems lost. The budget is out of control. The new CEO is a jerk. We're down 20 points at halftime.

At that moment, coaches are amazing. How many movies have we seen where a coach climbs on a chair in the locker room, shouts truth and inspirational cliches, and rallies the team? Or when someone in a failing company stands up and says we're not going to give up? Or as John Belushi said when he rose up and challenged his Animal House frat brothers to not give up, "Was it over when the Germans bombed Pearl Harbor? Nothing is over until we decide it is!"

Creating hope can come in a single moment when all hope seems lost, the end is near, and there's nothing left to do but give up. Cue the coach. Cue John Belushi.

Sometimes we find ourselves in a circumstance where hope for the future fails in a single intense moment. More often, it gives out in the hope-killing grind of daily life. Like when you set a goal to obtain a college degree, yet ending the quest sometimes seems like your only choice—until a friend challenges you to keep going. Or you train for a marathon, and along the way, the pain and aches make you want to give up—until a sports medicine doctor informs you that you just need to swap shoes, and your hope returns with a flourish. We all know those dark moments where all seems lost—until someone brings insights and you instantly feel hope return in force.

THINK AND DISCUSS (PART THREE)

- How do you see leaders create hope?
- How do you create hope?
- Who in your life needs you to create hope right now?
- How can you recognize that someone near to you needs their hope rekindled?

What about people who have given up hope for humanity?

Studies suggest that our brains function better and we feel physically better when the presence of hope lifts us through tough, challenging, and difficult situations. Whether dealing with adversity or uncertainty, we always do better with hope. But we have to work at having hope, and that hope often forms and grows as we connect with others.

At times if can feel as if we are surrounded by fellow humans who fear the world is going to end in nuclear war or decline into a dystopia ruled by rich people. No matter how they look at it, the future is bleak at best—so why bother?

Hope is a feeling, belief, and understanding that the future will be better. Hope also acknowledges that we sometimes first pass through worse things before we get to the better future. Yet I'm convinced that when we believe that the future will be better in some way, shape, or form, then together we can have a shared sense of hope. And we will get better. As a society. Together.

CHAPTER 23

Next Steps

Congratulations for getting this far!

Perhaps you read this book straight through, cover to cover. Perhaps you bounced around, reading the chapters that resonated with you. Perhaps you focused on a handful of topics. No matter how you got here, you did. Give yourself a pat on the back.

You have engaged in a journey of self-discovery that will get better and better. You are on your way to becoming a better person, teammate, and leader.

WHAT'S NEXT?

- If you answered the questions in your head as you read the chapters, go back and write down your answers. You've had time to process and reflect. Now it's time to put your answers on paper. It doesn't matter if writing is easy or hard for you, write something down.
- If you wrote down your answers by yourself, find a spouse, friend, partner, colleague, or anyone who you can engage with you in the questions. Share the questions with that person. Give yourself and your conversation partner time to process, then discuss your answers.
- If you talked with someone about the questions in each chapter, expand your group to three or four people. Find 15 minutes on

Monday and answer the first set of questions, then 15 minutes Wednesday for the second, and finally 15 minutes on Friday for the third set of questions. Take a week off, then start again with another chapter.

- If you have your group of three or four, attend a Ripple Intent Breakfast Club in your area to join the community. If there isn't one, read out to info@rippleintent.org to start one up.
- If you want to explore a topic with a group and want help to prepare, reach out to info@rippleintent.org
- Looking for more? Get a copy of the book, Powerful Conversations, for 21 more topics.
- If you want to have a conversation with me, call me at 970-744-8466.

We need to be intentional about having conversations that matter, and you having this book is the first step. By engaging ourselves and others in the journey of self-discovery, together we can make the world a better place—one conversation at a time.

www.ingramcontent.com/pod-product-compliance
Lightning Source LLC
Chambersburg PA
CBHW071550200326
41519CB00021BB/6678